The Roman Empire

Roots of Imperialism

Series Editors
Reinhard Bernbeck and Susan Pollock, Berlin/Binghamton

This series highlights the relevance of past empires for our contemporary world. It is concerned primarily with the political nature of connections between the past and the present. The approach is radical in that it directs the reader to a recognition of how past empires are theoretically and practically entangled in contemporary imperialist and economically exploitative endeavors.

The series sets itself apart from other books on past empires by including the point of view of dependent populations and victims of imperialism, rather than focusing solely on their beneficiaries, the well-known kings and imperators and their material surroundings of monuments and gold. Accordingly, the books devote attention to actions taken by dependent populations in response to imperial politics by giving a historical voice to resistance, subversion, and evasion.

The books also investigate the ways in which past empires survive – or, in some instances, are silenced - in present conditions. Residues of the past serve political ideologies in often hidden ways, making them all the more powerful because they are taken for granted. The books reveal imperialist, nationalist, neocolonialist or economic goals of powerholders today who mobilize past imperial figures and structures as well as their material remains to support their own agendas.

THE ROMAN EMPIRE

Roots of Imperialism

Neville Morley

PlutoPress
www.plutobooks.com

First published 2010 by Pluto Press
345 Archway Road, London N6 5AA and
175 Fifth Avenue, New York, NY 10010

www.plutobooks.com

Distributed in the United States of America exclusively by
Palgrave Macmillan, a division of St. Martin's Press LLC,
175 Fifth Avenue, New York, NY 10010

British Library Cataloguing in Publication Data
A catalogue record for this book is available from the British Library

ISBN   978 0 7453 2870 6   Hardback
ISBN   978 0 7453 2869 0   Paperback

Library of Congress Cataloging in Publication Data applied for

10   9   8   7   6   5   4   3   2   1

Designed and produced for Pluto Press by
Chase Publishing Services Ltd, 33 Livonia Road, Sidmouth, EX10 9JB, England
Typeset from disk by Stanford DTP Services, Northampton, England
Printed and bound in the European Union by
CPI Antony Rowe, Chippenham and Eastbourne

For Hugh

Contents

Acknowledgements

This book is dedicated to the memory of my uncle, Hugh Chapman, who as an archaeologist and museum curator first inspired my interest in the messy and fragmentary reality of the past, rather than its polished and misleading representation. I have no idea what he might have made of my take on the subject; this is an inadequate substitute for all the conversations that we might have had.

As ever, my greatest debt of gratitude is to Anne, for putting up once again with the agonies of book-writing and for helping to pull me through them. I have as always been inspired by the ideas of numerous colleagues, both through conversation and through their publications, and particularly wish to mention Sue Alcock, Richard Alston, Clifford Ando, Catharine Edwards, David Grewal, Richard Hingley, Martin Jehne, David Mattingly, Jörg Rüpke, Nic Terrenato, Tim Whitmarsh and Greg Woolf. I am grateful to the University of Bristol for a year's research leave in which to complete the work and to recover from eight years' worth of faculty administration, to Gillian Clark for moral support, and to everyone on the 'Spill for providing a regular distraction.

Timeline

66–70:	Jewish revolt and subsequent war
115–17:	Second Jewish revolt
122:	Construction of Hadrian's Wall
167:	The Antonine Plague sweeps the empire
284–305:	Diocletian restores order after 50 years of political upheaval, and divides the empire in two
312:	Constantine seizes power in the west and declares his support of Christianity
361–63:	Pagan revival under Julian is cut short by his death
378:	A Roman army is defeated at Adrianople by the Goths
395:	Empire permanently divided after the death of Theodosius
410:	Sack of Rome by Alaric the Goth
439:	Carthage seized by the Vandals
476:	The last emperor in the west, Romulus Augustulus, is deposed

Introduction:
'Empire Without End'

I place no limits on them of time or space; I have given them power without boundaries.

(Virgil, *Aeneid*, I.278–9)

A millennium and a half after the end of the period of its unquestioned dominance, Rome remains a significant presence in Western culture. This is not only a matter of its continuing popularity as a setting for pseudo-historical drama in film and television, an exotic world of well-oiled gladiators, decadent emperors, seductive priestesses and political intrigue tempered with violence.[1] Since the Renaissance, Rome has had a prominent role in intellectual developments, in debates about the organisation of the state and the conduct of its foreign policy and about the nature and morality of encounters between Europe and the rest of the world.[2] Rome is seen as the greatest civilisation of the past, with a direct genetic and historical connection to Europe and the West, and hence stands as both an inspiration and a challenge to modernity. Even as the nineteenth century congratulated itself on its unprecedented material power – as Karl Marx put it in the *Communist Manifesto*, '[the modern bourgeoisie] has accomplished marvels wholly different from Egyptian pyramids, Roman aqueducts and Gothic cathedrals' – it was haunted by two fears: that in other respects it might have failed to match its ancient rival, and that it would prove no more able to escape the corrupting effects of time and success than Rome had done.[3] Modernity defined itself against antiquity, drawing on the tradition of engagement with its literature and history and on the idea of Rome developed in art and literature over the centuries, and measured its achievements against those past glories.

THE EXEMPLARY EMPIRE

In these debates Rome was understood in different ways, depending on what sort of comparison or contrast with the present was intended: discussions of political structures, such as Machiavelli's

1

The Prince or the debates around the United States constitution, considered Rome as a state, while advocates of a European or Western identity saw it as a civilisation. Most often, it was seen as an empire; indeed, as the archetypal empire, the epitome and supreme expression of imperial power. Later European empires sought to emphasise their connection to Rome, as a means of establishing their historical status and legitimising their dominance of others, and also derided the claims of other states, such as Byzantium.[4] The wish to claim a special relationship with the Roman Empire recurs time and again, from the insistence of the Carolingian kings on being styled 'emperor and Augustus' to the public pronouncements of the Holy Roman Empire, from the French and British empires of the nineteenth century to the Fascist and Nazi projects of the twentieth century.[5] Modern empires drew on Rome above all for their iconography, finding there the art and architecture considered appropriate to reflect and magnify imperial power. In capital cities such as Paris and London, in the government buildings designed by Lutyens in New Delhi and in the triumphal arches that are found in places that were never Roman settlements, such as Munich, or never even part of the Roman Empire, such as Berlin, the use of classical templates and styles both imitated the Roman deployment of monumental architecture as a means of domination and asserted a claim to be their rightful heirs.[6]

As well as providing the template for how an empire ought to present itself, Rome was central to modern debates about the nature, dynamics and morality of imperialism. Its status as an empire was beyond question; however 'empire' or 'imperialism' were defined, it was taken for granted that the definition would have to apply to Rome and, for the most part, the different definitions were derived from direct consideration of the Roman example.[7] References to the Roman Empire were ubiquitous in French and British discussions of empires (their own and their rivals') from the late eighteenth century; Rome, it was argued, represented a case that was sufficiently similar to contemporary experience to be worth considering.

> The Spanish Empire in America as it stood in the sixteenth and seventeenth centuries was still vaster in area [than the Roman Empire], as is the Russian Empire in Asia today. But the population of Spanish America was extremely small in comparison with that of the Roman Empire or that of India, and its organization much looser and less elaborate... Of all the dominions which the ancient world saw, it is only that of Rome that can well be compared with

any modern civilized State... So when we wish to examine the methods and the results of British rule in India by the light of any other dominion exercised under conditions even remotely similar, it is to the Roman Empire of the centuries between Augustus and Honorius that we must go.[8]

Besides these pragmatic arguments, there is a clear sense in many of these accounts that Rome, unlike Spain or Russia, is a worthy comparison for a modern European power; it is frequently claimed that there is not only a plausible analogy between the ancient and modern empire but also a direct genetic link (most plausibly asserted in the case of Mussolini's Italy, but the same assertion was made in France and even Britain) or a special affinity (the favoured British approach).

The comparison was never wholly straightforward; rather as the Italian Fascists tempered their classicism with futurism and a fervent belief in technological progress, so British and French writers evoked Rome less as a model to be imitated slavishly than as the basis for dialogue and debate. Sometimes the Roman example was brought forward as a basis for criticism of contemporary policies, as Edmund Burke compared the British in Ireland with the Romans in Gaul and praised the latter for mitigating the violence of conquest with intermarriage and civilisation, or Alexander de Tocqueville contrasted the Romans' tolerance of diversity amongst their subjects with the actions of the French in Algeria.[9] Rome's role in bringing civilisation to the barbarians was cited time and again, especially in the context of British rule in India ('an Empire similar to that of Rome, in which we hold the position not merely of a ruling but of an educating and civilising race') and, from the mid-nineteenth century, questions about what lessons might be learned from Rome were a fixture on the entrance examination for the India Civil Service.[10] The idea that Roman policy towards its dominions was coherent, pragmatic and advantageous for all involved was put forward by Adam Smith in the eighteenth century with regard to the American colonies, and was still being asserted well into the twentieth; for example, the Earl of Cromer claimed in 1910, 'something of the clearness of political vision and bluntness of expression which characterized the Imperialists of Ancient Rome might, not without advantage, be imparted to our own Imperialist policy'.[11]

Alternatively, Rome might be considered in order to emphasise the achievements of the modern empire: its greater geographical extent, its dominion over greater numbers of people, its ability to raise up new nations from its colonists (but not, of course, from its native subjects). The Christian identity of modern imperialism was frequently cited as the basis of its superiority, bringing true enlightenment to the barbarians rather than the vague agnosticism of the Roman Empire: 'One must not speak of toleration as the note of its policy, because there was nothing to tolerate. All religions were equally true, or equally useful, each for its own country or nation... Nobody thought of converting the devotees of crocodiles or cats.'[12] The assertion of technological and spiritual progress was not only a matter of measuring the modern achievement against the ancient; there was also the pressing concern to demonstrate that history was or could be progressive and that the Empire – or Western civilisation as a whole – was not fated to follow the Romans on the path of corruption and dissolution, decline and fall.[13] Roman history offered a view of the entire life cycle of a civilisation, and many writers sought to identify the lessons that ought to be learnt and the mistakes that must be avoided in order to escape this apparently inevitable fate. This was not just a matter of considering the final centuries of the Empire; in Britain and the United States in particular, great attention was paid to the circumstances that led to the fall of the Roman Republic and the establishment of autocracy, with concerns about the association between empire in the sense of territorial dominion and empire as despotism surfacing both in the face of Napoleon's imperial pretensions and in debates about the constitutional implications of proclaiming Victoria as Empress of India.[14]

Commentators on empire sought precedents, examples and vocabulary from the past to make sense of their own situation, both the encounter with new peoples and situations, and the impact of this on their own society. Whereas in most contexts the 'horizon of expectation' had moved ever further away from the 'space of experience', creating the sense that the present was vastly different from the past and that the future would be more different still and thus discrediting the claims of history to offer any useful guidance for present situations, this particular aspect of the experience of modernity did not appear to be so entirely unprecedented.[15] Indeed, Rome came to seem more relevant as modern empires finally matched its achievements and it ceased to be perceived as a unique development. More analytical approaches to the study of 'empire' and 'imperialism' as political, social and economic phenomena adopted a similar perspective, identifying analogies between historical empires as the basis for deriving a transhistorical definition – and almost inevitably taking Rome as their key example.[16]

Even those theories which asserted the existence of an unbridgeable gap between past and present, seeing imperialism as a phenomenon specific to modern capitalism rather than as a universal human tendency, retained Rome as a touchstone. Such writers took their cue from Karl Marx in rejecting attempts at identifying modern values and institutions in the past, thereby naturalising and universalising them and denying the possibility of any radical alternative; as Bukharin argued in his analysis of imperialism in the world economy, 'The aim in this case is clear. The futility of the ideas of labour democracy must be "proven" by placing it on a level with the lumpen proletariat, the workers and the artisans of antiquity.'[17] They also echoed Marx in the fact that, nevertheless, classical references recur repeatedly, despite their ostensible irrelevance to any analysis of the modern world.[18] Rome became the symbol of the failures and atrocities of imperialism, rather than its greatness, as for Marx it had been the obvious analogy for the failures and atrocities of modernity: 'there exist symptoms of decay, far surpassing the horrors recorded of the latter times of the Roman Empire'.[19] Far from showing that imperialism was inevitable, as a natural expression of the human instinct to dominate and conquer, Rome pointed to the eventual dissolution of any such attempt at dominating others.

This is the largest, plainest instance history presents of the social parasitic process by which a moneyed interest within the State, usurping the reins of government, makes for imperial expansion in order to fasten economic suckers into foreign bodies so as to drain them of their wealth in order to support domestic luxury. The new Imperialism differs in no vital point from this old example. The element of political tribute is now absent or quite subsidiary, and the crudest forms of slavery have disappeared: some elements of more genuine and disinterested government serve to qualify and mask the distinctively parasitic nature of the later sort. But nature is not mocked: the laws which, operative throughout nature, doom the parasite to atrophy, decay, and final extinction, are not evaded by nations any more than by individual organisms. The greater complexity of the modern process, the endeavour to escape the parasitic reaction by rendering some real but quite unequal and inadequate services to 'the host', may retard but cannot finally avert the natural consequences of living upon others.[20]

THE NEW ROME?

That's not the way the world really works any more. We're an empire now, and when we act, we create our own reality. And while you're studying that reality – judiciously, as you will – we'll act again, creating other new realities, which you can study too, and that's how things will sort out.[21]

The same dynamic of debate has been seen in discussions of the much-disputed 'new imperialism' of the United States and its collaborators. The template for the empire that shapes the world in its own image – to the confusion of the 'reality-based community' – is of course Rome, and even in the early twentieth century, despite the long tradition in the United States of the rejection of overt imperialism in the name of liberty, claims were being made that the United States was becoming the New Rome by building upon the example of the old one.[22]

By adding to what we may call the scientific legacy of past imperialisms the initiative born of its own inspiration and surroundings, this great nation has subverted every principle in the sphere of politics, just as it had already transformed them in the sphere of material progress.[23]

In the last twenty years, the argument that the USA should be compared with Rome rather than with any other empire – and, more importantly, that this comparison highlights the desirability of imperial power, whereas empires such as the British or the Spanish exemplify its negative aspects – has become something of a cliché.[24] Rome is cited in attempts at rebranding imperialism as the expansion of civilisation and protection for oppressed minorities, with the emphasis on 'soft power' rather than military force – with the extension of the Latin language under Rome offered as a reassuring analogy for the global dominance of English and Hollywood movies.[25] Rome shows that empire brings stability through its unprecedented dominance and hence bestows peace, law, order, education and prosperity on the regions it dominates.[26] The characters of the Romans and Americans are compared, as the explanation for their global dominance: 'What unites both are their untamed energy, their determination to carry something out to its logical conclusion, and their conviction that anything can be achieved if one only invests enough energy.'[27]

As in the debates around British imperialism, Rome is not evoked solely as a direct analogy for the United States. Some writers are equally interested in the differences between the two, seen as essential for understanding the likely fate of the modern empire:

> We live in a world that has no precedent since the age of the later Roman emperors. It is not just the military domination of the world by a single power. Nor is it even the awesome reach of this capability. Nor is it just the display of resolve... The Roman parallels are evident, with the difference that the Romans were untroubled by an imperial destiny, while the Americans have had an empire since Teddy Roosevelt, yet persist in believing they do not.[28]

For some, the example of Rome points the way forward for the United States, to seize its imperial destiny; for others, it highlights likely threats to American dominance and so indicates the need for shifts in policy:

> The United States may be more powerful than any other polity since the Roman Empire, but like Rome, America is neither invincible nor invulnerable. Rome did not succumb to the rise of another empire, but to the onslaught of waves of barbarians. Modern high-tech terrorists are the new barbarians.[29]

Finally, many writers seek to identify the unique elements in the United States constitution or spirit that will enable it to escape the fate of Rome, resisting dissolution and corruption. However, even an insistence on American exceptionalism, its manifest destiny and its freedom from the usual dynamics of rise and fall, does not negate the power of Rome as the great comparison and the archetypal empire: 'Imagine a gauge of imperial character on which Rome scores 10.'[30] For Niall Ferguson, despite all his cheer-leading for American power, Rome is likely to remain the United States' great rival for the foreseeable future:

> Like Rome, it began with a relatively small core... Like Rome, it was an inclusive empire, relatively (though not wholly) promiscuous in the way that it conferred citizenship. Like Rome,

it had, at least for a time, its disenfranchised slaves. But unlike Rome, its republican constitution has withstood the ambitions of any would-be Caesars – so far. (It is of course early days. The United States is 228 years old. When Caesar crossed the Rubicon in 49 BC, the Roman Republic was 460 years old).[31]

It is notable that all these writers focus on the balance between the positive impact of empire on the world and its potentially negative impact on the imperial society; the same is true of accounts that take Rome as a model for the benign impact of globalisation under the direction of international institutions of law and exchange.[32] There are some discussions that take a less optimistic view of Rome's influence; mention of Rome in the context of the European Union, for example, is in most cases intended to underpin furious denunciations of the imposition of a single system of currency, the iniquities of European human rights legislation and the destruction of national identity – where not simply asserting that the European Union's ambition to make itself the new Roman Empire is a sign of imminent Apocalypse.[33] Hardt and Negri's monumental *Empire* takes Rome as the model for the all-encompassing world order, generating its own basis of legitimacy by presenting its order as permanent, eternal and necessary; their critique, and their vision for the future, is heavily based on ancient analysis of the workings and failures of empire.[34] Both of these examples echo the standard image of Rome as all-powerful and totalising, shaping its empire as it wished; they simply re-evaluate the impact of that power. Similarly, the criticism of United States policy in Iraq by the journalist Robert Fisk, asking what the Romans would have made of it (answer: a hopeless failure; the Americans are the real barbarians), reinforces the inherited image.[35]

Most critics of modern imperialism have focused on its impact on the societies that have been colonised or invaded rather than considering its historical antecedents. The reason is obvious: there is a risk that historical parallels can serve to legitimise present-day actions, as the proponents of American power clearly intend them to do. The image of the Roman Empire as the bringer of peace, order, prosperity and civilisation to the conquered provinces may be too well entrenched in Western culture for it to be able to support the criticism of imperialism in general, rather than criticism of the failures of a specific imperialism that falls short of Roman achievements. The example of Rome, it is implied, shows that not all interventions by a superior power are destructive or illegitimate;

it offers an alibi for the admitted failures and atrocities of other empires, making the case that this time things can be different. The attempted rehabilitation of the British Empire, however historically plausible, will always be controversial and so of limited use in gathering support for current policy; the Roman Empire is a 'safe' example because no one is likely to protest against its positive image on the grounds that their ancestors were slaughtered or enslaved. That does not mean it has no power; on the contrary, because of centuries of reverence for Roman culture and achievements, Rome remains a powerful symbol of the majesty and glories of empire.

Clearly, however, this image of Roman achievement is extremely partial and misleading, cherry-picking the most positive aspects and air-brushing the violence and inequality on which they were founded. Like the Rome of Hollywood movies, it is a fictional construct based mainly on the monuments of architecture and literary culture, decorated with touches of the exotic and transgressive. A striking example of this is a remark made by Benjamin Disraeli in a speech of 1879:

> One of the greatest of the Romans, when asked what were his politics, replied, *Imperium et libertas*. That would not make a bad programme for a British Ministry. It is one from which Her Majesty's advisers do not shrink.[36]

In fact, the quotation is a fiction; no Roman ever said that, but, whether or not Disraeli was conscious of his invention, the line works because it accords with our expectations and image of the Roman Empire.

The Rome to which apologists for empire refer is presented as a stable, known object which can easily be compared in all its facets with modern experiences, but this is an illusion. Our actual knowledge of Rome is fragmentary and sometimes contradictory, with every statement needing to be qualified or questioned; the labour of scholars since the eighteenth century has tended to multiply uncertainties rather than establish certainties as growing understanding of the way modern societies work has highlighted our ignorance about the operations of Roman society. Furthermore, the history of Rome spans at least a millennium and a half, and the history of its overseas empire in Western Europe covers more than 750 years. It was, of course, far more stable than any modern society, but it still changed significantly during that time, and can be reduced to a single and straightforward image of 'the Roman

Empire' only through drastic simplification, either concentrating on a particular period (as many accounts focus either on the virtuous Republic or on the peaceful empire of the Principate) or creating a composite image that never existed in reality. Of course, the writers employing Rome for analytical or rhetorical purposes have little use for such academic pedantry, since it undermines the usefulness of the example; for all that their arguments draw strength from the supposed reality of their historical evidence, they are really deploying the modern conception of 'Rome' rather than its reality. This is one reason why the Roman Empire is worth studying: not as a means of understanding better how to run an empire and dominate other countries, or of finding a justification for humanitarian or military intervention, but as a means of understanding and questioning modern conceptions of empire and imperialism, and the way they are deployed in contemporary political debates.

The relationship between ideas of the past and present conceptions is not one-sided; just as developing historical understanding of Rome influenced modern ideas about empire and the encounter with other cultures, so those modern ideas and experiences influenced understanding of the ancient world, through the questions that scholars asked of their material and the ideas that they brought to bear in its interpretation. The obvious example is the concept of the 'Romanisation' of the provinces, which developed out of questions about the nature of cultural change in Britain under Roman rule that were directly inspired by British experiences in India. Recent studies of the uses of this concept in ancient history and archaeology reveal how those contemporary influences led to one-sided readings of the ancient evidence, over-emphasising the role of the Roman state in imposing change and neglecting the active role of the provincials.[37] There has also been a tendency to see Roman imperialism as a coherent and directed process, because that is what the experience of later empires (which sought in part deliberately to recreate the Roman empire) led scholars to expect to find in their sources; further, there is the habit of regarding its development as inevitable, on the basis of theories that see imperialism as the outcome of natural human tendencies.[38] Classical studies were, or became, an imperialist enterprise shaped by empire and working to sustain it, both through their role in the education of the governing elite and by providing the foundation for the claims of the West to possess a superior civilisation. For the most part, until very recently, ancient historians and literary scholars have been in complete denial of this: not only of the dependence of their interpretations on ideas and conceptions shaped by the West's encounter with other cultures but also of the role of empire and its requirements in determining what was recovered from the classical past, shaping what was excavated and collected as well as what questions were asked of the material.[39] The study of post-colonial classics, the academic equivalent of literary works such as Derek Walcott's *Omeros*, exploring the role of the classical legacy in European imperial projects, is a very recent development.

ROOTS OF IMPERIALISM

The aim of this book is to consider, and establish a dialogue between, the three facets of the encounter between Roman and modern imperialism: the way that images of classical antiquity have been shaped by modern experiences of imperialism and colonialism; the way that modern discourses on imperialism, globalisation and modernisation have been shaped by the eternally contested image of Rome; and the way that modern scholarly interpretations of Roman imperialism, when the constant dialogue and reciprocal influence between past and present are taken properly into account, may be able to illuminate the dynamics, consequences and trajectories of modern imperialism. The last of these is probably the most contentious, given the vast differences between antiquity and modernity in terms of technology, knowledge and social organisation; if we have imperialism at all in the contemporary world – a much-debated point – it must be a very different sort of imperialism, and analogies with the Roman Empire must, as illustrated above, always be suspect. Nevertheless, historical analogies can illuminate through contrast as much as comparison; the study of an alien culture and its particular approach to issues that persist today – most obviously, the management of diversity, the globalisation of culture and the nature of economic development – may throw aspects of the modern world into sharper relief. If nothing else, a fuller understanding of how the Roman Empire really worked offers a defence against the tendentious claims of contemporary apologists for Western dominance.

This is unavoidably a partial, personal and somewhat polemical account of several equally vast and controversial subjects. The aim here is to offer an introduction to the most important themes in the study of the origins, nature and impact of Roman imperialism. This is not a narrative history of the Roman Empire: that is partly due to the author's preference for analysis and a wish to understand the underlying logic and dynamics of economic, social, cultural and political systems; partly due to a feeling that the market is already over-burdened with narrative accounts; and partly due to a basic ideological suspicion of that sort of history, at least in the case of Rome. The power of narrative is precisely that it does not make its interpretative assumptions and judgements explicit, but simply tells a story; in this instance, it is all too easy and common for narrative histories of the Roman Empire to present its triumph, ever so subtly, as an inevitable progress (as the Romans themselves tended to) or as the outcome of mere chance in battle and political debate (as many modern commentators imply). For a full understanding of the history of Rome, this book needs to be read in conjunction with one or more such narratives (see the section on Further Reading for some suggestions). The test of any interpretation is whether it can make sense of the succession of individual events – but equally the connections between events are invented (rather than found) by the historian on the basis of their conceptual framework and presuppositions. The issues discussed in this book should offer some indication of what ideas and issues may underlie the particular choices of emphasis and interpretation in any narrative of the Empire's history.

Even in selecting themes for analysis, it has been necessary to focus on certain aspects of particular topics rather than attempting to offer a comprehensive account, and decisions about what is most important are inevitably based on ideological as much as on pragmatic grounds. Two issues are particularly important in this regard. Firstly, there is the balance to be struck between the nature of the surviving evidence and the importance of doing justice to the whole of Roman society. The majority of historical sources for the Roman Empire were produced by or for the educated ruling elite, and speak almost exclusively of their experiences and attitudes. The evidence for the lives of the mass of the population, including the provincial subjects of Rome, is predominantly archaeological and so offers more insights about some aspects of their lives – the material conditions of their existence, most obviously – than about their thoughts or experiences. An account based solely on the material evidence would have little to say about the dynamics of the political, economic and social systems that shaped the lives of the population of the Roman Empire; an account based solely on the literary and epigraphic sources would say next to nothing about the lives of the vast majority, and would tend to take many questionable aspects of Roman life entirely for granted – but it would be full of colour and incident, which is why the majority of earlier accounts of the Roman Empire have, indeed, offered such a perspective.

Secondly, there is the all-encompassing nature of Roman imperialism: without its empire, Rome would not have been Rome as we know it. All aspects of Roman society were permeated and influenced by the acquisition of empire, at least by the time that historical sources began to be produced; our knowledge of pre-imperial Rome is shaped by the perceptions, and nostalgia, of the imperial era. An account of the Roman empire is arguably an account of the entirety of Roman civilisation, a task far beyond a book of this size; my aim here is to focus as far as possible on the dynamics of imperialism and its immediate consequences, especially those aspects which either drew the attention of later writers on imperialism, such as the changes in the culture and society of the conquered provinces, or which seem to have something to say about contemporary concerns, such as the economic development of the empire. From the dynamics of the Roman conquest of the world (Chapter 1), the nature of Roman rule (Chapter 2), the economic impact of empire (Chapter 3) and the social and cultural influence of Rome (Chapter 4) to the collapse of the Roman system and its aftermath (Envoi), the example of Rome has shaped our modern conceptions of 'civilisation' and what happens when that civilisation meets another, apparently alien, culture. It is Rome above all that leads us to view those outside our culture as barbarians who must be compelled to conform to our expectations of thought and behaviour, or else feared and mistrusted as a threat to the foundations of our civilisation.[40]

In Virgil's *Aeneid*, one of the key texts of Roman identity, Jupiter promises the Romans power – *imperium*, the word from which we derive 'empire' – without limits of time or space.[41] The idea of Rome has long outlived the physical empire that gave it form, and now holds sway over vastly more people and a far greater geographical area than the Romans ever ruled. It continues to shape our understanding of the nature of imperialism and, thus, however subtly, to influence the workings of the world. From a purely historical point of view, other empires have an equal claim to our attention: China, Persia, the Mughals, the Mayans and the Aztecs. However, the reason why historians have devoted so much attention to Rome and disparaged the claims of other empires, the way that Rome has been claimed as one of the foundations of our entire civilisation, is precisely why we need to keep studying it: the Roman Empire is still ruling us, and we need to understand our rulers and their system to liberate ourselves.

1
'Carthage Must Be Destroyed': The Dynamics of Roman Imperialism

It is said that Cato contrived to drop a Libyan fig in the middle of the Senate, as he shook out the folds of his toga, and then, as the senators were admiring its size and beauty, said that the country where it grew was only three days' sailing from Rome. And in one thing he was even more savage, namely, in concluding his opinion on any question whatsoever with the words: 'In my opinion, Carthage must be destroyed'.

(Plutarch, *Life of Cato the Elder*, 27.1)

In 149 BCE, the Roman senate despatched an army to Africa: the city of Carthage had broken the terms of the peace treaty it had signed 60 years earlier, by starting a war with the neighbouring kingdom of Numidia without Roman permission, and therefore had to be punished.[1] The Carthaginians, having failed to persuade the senate of the justice of their grievances against the Numidians (having, indeed, endured 60-odd years of unprovoked harassment, with Rome almost invariably deciding against them whenever they complained), sought to avert catastrophe by committing themselves to the faith of the Romans, an unconditional surrender of their whole territory and population. Their ambassadors were told that the proposal was acceptable, and that the Carthaginians would be granted their freedom and the possession of their whole territory, provided that they handed over 300 hostages, the sons of leading citizens, and obeyed the orders of the consuls who were commanding the army. Those unspecified orders, it transpired, were firstly to hand over all the weapons in the city; when that had been done, the Carthaginians were then ordered to abandon their city and establish a new settlement, at least ten miles from the sea.

The motive for this was transparent, as was made clear in the speech that the Greek historian Appian placed in the mouth of the Roman general: the absolute destruction of Carthage and the basis of its historic power.

If we were addressing you as enemies, people of Carthage, it would be necessary only to speak and then use force, but since this is a matter of the common good (somewhat of our own, and still more of yours), I have no objection to giving you the reasons, if you may thus be persuaded instead of being coerced. The sea reminds you of the dominion and power you once acquired by means of it. It prompts you to wrong-doing, and brings you to grief. By means of the sea you invaded Sicily and lost it again. Then you invaded Spain and were driven out of it. While a treaty was in force you plundered merchants on the sea, and ours especially, and in order to conceal the crime you threw them overboard, until finally you were caught at it and then gave us Sardinia by way of penalty. Thus you lost Sardinia also by means of this sea, which always begets a grasping disposition by the very facilities which it offers for gain. (Appian, *The Punic Wars*, 86)

As Appian certainly assumed his readers knew, a Carthaginian or a Greek would have offered a very different account of the events of the previous century and a half. The two earlier Punic Wars between Rome and Carthage, 264–241 BCE and 218–201 BCE, could equally well be seen as the inevitable result of two major powers coming into direct contact with one another, each fearing the other. The first war broke out after a group of mercenaries seized control of Messana in Sicily, and appealed to both Rome and Carthage for assistance against the attempts of the powerful city of Syracuse to re-take it; the Carthaginians responded promptly by installing a garrison in Messana, whereupon the Romans feared that Carthaginian dominance of Sicily might threaten their own hegemony in Italy and belatedly decided to send their own forces. In Roman accounts, this was a purely defensive move, in response to a request for help; the eventual acquisition of Sicily and Sardinia as overseas territories was more or less an accidental outcome of their concern to defend justice and protect their own rights. A Carthaginian would have emphasised the way in which the upstart Italian power was clearly seeking to extend its reach into areas that were traditionally part of their own sphere of influence in the western Mediterranean, inciting proxy wars and finding pretexts for military intervention.

The outbreak of the Second Punic War offers an example. Carthage was above all a naval power, founded by the Phoenicians whose ships had traded across the Mediterranean for centuries; it sought to establish colonies in regions, such as southern Spain, which could supply timber and metal for its ships. During the uneasy peace after 241 BCE, it increased its hold on this area. The Roman response to the threat of a revival in their rival's power was initially to make an agreement that the Carthaginians would remain south of the river Ebro; then, in the late 220s BCE, they established a relationship with the town of Saguntum, in the heart of that territory. With the promise of Roman protection, the Saguntines seized the opportunity to attack a neighbouring community and were punished by Hannibal, whereupon the Romans issued a blanket ultimatum: hand over the general or face war. The immediate consequences were disastrous for Rome, as Hannibal crossed the Alps and defeated a series of Roman generals in Italy, but the conclusion of the war was the reduction of Carthage from a world power to a minor state, forbidden to make war without Roman permission and required to pay a hefty indemnity to Rome for 60 years, while Rome added Spain to its overseas territories and now enjoyed undisputed mastery of the western Mediterranean.

Carthage remained a prosperous city, with rich agricultural resources and thriving trade connections; some Romans became convinced that, despite the loss of its empire, it would always be a threat to their security. According to the contemporary Greek historian Polybius (36.2), they simply waited for a suitable pretext that would persuade other nations that they acted honourably; the Carthaginians' breach of the treaty conditions presented the opportunity to destroy their naval capacity, the basis of their old empire and of the future empire that the Romans feared or professed to fear, once and for all. Faced with the prospect of having their city destroyed in order to save it from itself, the Carthaginian response to the ultimatum was to fight; despite having given up their weapons, they successfully resisted the Roman army until 146 BCE. By then, the majority of the population had died of starvation or in battle; the remainder – numbers are notoriously unreliable in ancient sources, but the figure of 50,000 is cited – were sold into slavery, as was customary. The city burned for days and was then abandoned. The story that the fields were then sown with salt, to destroy their fertility and prevent anyone from living there, is a fabrication first encountered in the nineteenth century; the Romans, rather more practically, declared the territory to be public land, redistributed it to a mixture of local farmers and Italian settlers, and established it as the new province of Africa, paying a regular tribute to Rome.[2]

APPROACHING ROMAN IMPERIALISM

The Third Punic War was one of many fought by Rome in the course of its rise to the status of a world empire, from the conquest of its immediate neighbour Veii in 396 BCE, through the subjugation of the rival empires of Carthage, Macedon (168 BCE), Syria (63 BCE) and Egypt (30 BCE), to the invasion of Britain in 43 CE. While not every war resulted in the expansion of its power, let alone in the acquisition of new territory, the long-term trend was unmistakable. The obvious line of investigation is the nature of this persistent aggression and drive to conquer, the origins and dynamics of Roman imperialism. Surprisingly, however, a number of objections have been raised to thinking about the subject in these terms.

There is no Latin equivalent of 'imperialism'.[3] The word *imperium*, from which both 'imperialism' and 'empire' derive, referred originally to the power possessed by a Roman magistrate to command and expect obedience. It came, in time, to be extended to the power of the Roman people as a whole and then to that of the emperor, and took on a further meaning as the area within which Rome expected to exert its dominance without any opposition: its empire. However, the development of ideas about the nature of Rome's overseas dominions followed long after they had actually been acquired, rather than preceding or influencing the process of conquest and annexation. Even in retrospect, Roman authors did not conceive of their city's rise to dominance as the result of a policy, let alone as the result of greed or ambition, but rather as the reward of virtue and wise decision-making, along with the favour of the gods and the occasional piece of good fortune.[4] According to Cicero, Rome fought only just wars undertaken in the face of provocation and in defence of its safety or its honour (for example, defending one of its allies), having always first offered the enemy an opportunity to make reparations instead. The acquisition of an empire was simply the result of Roman success in such virtuous endeavours, from its dominance of the league of local powers in Latium in the fourth century and triumph over Carthage in the third, to the acquisition of vast domains in Gaul and the eastern Mediterranean thereafter: 'our people, by defending their allies, have gained dominion over the whole world' (*Republic*, II.34).

The absence of any Roman term for a policy or ideology of expansion persuaded some modern historians to take such self-serving claims, and the rituals which the Romans undertook before a formal declaration of war – above all, the issuing of a non-negotiable ultimatum – entirely at face value.[5] Roman behaviour was thus characterised as 'defensive imperialism', a view which also allowed Rome to be taken as a positive model and justification for empire-building. In sixteenth-century Spanish debates about the justice of the conquests in America, 'the example of the Romans, whose rule over other peoples was just and legitimate' was cited regularly in defence of Spanish imperialism, and this argument rested on the assertion that Rome had expanded 'by taking over by law of war the cities and provinces of enemies from whom they had received an injury'.[6] Centuries later, the Earl of Cromer, identifying various analogies between the Roman and British empires, noted:

> That in proceeding from conquest to conquest each step in advance was in ancient, as it has been in modern, times accompanied by misgivings, and was often taken with a reluctance that was by no means feigned; that Rome, equally with the modern expansive powers, more especially Great Britain and Russia, was impelled onwards by the imperious and irresistible necessity of acquiring defensible frontiers; that the public opinion of the world scoffed 2,000 years ago, as it does now, at the alleged necessity; and that each onward move was attributed to an insatiable lust for extended dominion.[7]

Because Roman imperialism had, according to unimpeachable ancient sources, been defensive and reasonable, it was entirely credible to ignore the criticism and to believe that British imperialism might be the same.

Although few historians would now hold the view that Roman wars were invariably or even frequently defensive, the use of the term 'imperialism' in the analysis of Roman expansion remains controversial; it may be mentioned only to be rejected, or omitted altogether, even if the author is happy to attribute less than noble motives to the Romans.[8] The reasons for this vary and are not always stated. Some historians understand 'imperialism' strictly as an ideology of expansionism that must be consciously held and explicitly proclaimed by the conquering state, conditions which clearly did not apply to Rome. For others, the modern connotations of the term, pejorative and highly political, imply that its application to the ancient world will inevitably result in anachronism. There is a long-standing tradition in ancient history of rejecting all modern concepts and theories as misleading, claiming that they force the reality of the past into conformity with modern assumptions and expectations, and ignore its specificity and detail in favour of broad generalisations.[9] To think about Roman history in terms of 'imperialism' is, according to this argument, to see it solely in terms of the dynamics of modern empires, driven by capitalist over-accumulation, or nationalism and racism, or competition between modern states. Rather, we should focus on the detail of events – the reasons why the Romans went to war in individual cases and the outcomes of those wars – without any suggestion that this was a coherent or directed process and without recourse to modern concepts.

> If, therefore, we hope to understand the groping, stumbling, accidental expansion of Rome, we must rid ourselves of anachronistic generalizations and 'remote causes' and look instead for the specific accidents that led the nation unwittingly from one contest to another until, to her own surprise, Rome was mistress of the Mediterranean.[10]

The flaws in such arguments are obvious. The fact that Roman expansionism was not an explicit policy clearly does not mean that the growth of the empire was entirely accidental; on the contrary, the fact that the Romans consistently failed to get on with their neighbours, and as a result steadily accumulated more territory, suggests that it was anything but. Doing away with modern terms of analysis does not enable historians to escape from the way that, consciously or subconsciously, their interpretations are inevitably shaped by contemporary conceptions and concerns. It is certainly the case that 'imperialism' has political connotations, generally but not invariably negative, and that applying the term to Rome is intended to establish links between past and present – but an insistence on avoiding the word, refusing to draw any connections between comparable historical events and denying the existence of the phenomenon can be equally political, offering an alibi for Roman imperialism and for imperialism in general. The idea of an 'accidental' empire, acquired 'in a fit of absence of mind' or as the entirely unforeseen consequence of entirely reasonable actions, was just as useful to apologists for the British Empire as the idea of an empire acquired in justifiable self-defence.[11]

> The Roman Empire was founded upon military considerations… This does not mean that their Empire was purely the outcome of deliberate conquest and annexation on a preconceived plan. They were drawn on in the path of Empire, as we have been drawn on, by force of circumstances.[12]

At the same time, of course, there are certainly risks in taking too simplistic or monolithic a view of 'imperialism', obscuring all historical difference; in many important respects, the process of Roman expansion was significantly different from that of the Spanish or British, or late-twentieth-century United States hegemony. This may be a concern not only for historians but also for studies of contemporary imperialism. Writers in the Marxist tradition have long been aware of the dangers of understanding 'imperialism' in excessively general, transhistorical terms, as a 'policy of conquest in general', defined above all by its past historical manifestations and thus obscuring the specific nature, roots and dynamics of the modern phenomenon. As Nikolai Bukharin argued,

> From this point of view one can speak with equal right of Alexander the Macedonian's and the Spanish conquerors' imperialism, of the imperialism of Carthage and Ivan III, of ancient Rome and modern America, of Napoleon and Hindenburg. Simple as this theory may be, it is absolutely untrue. It is untrue because it 'explains' everything, i.e. it explains absolutely nothing![13]

'Publicists and scholars attempt to paint modern imperialism as something akin to the policies of the heroes of antiquity with their "imperium"', ignoring the fundamental differences between ancient slave society and modern capitalism.[14] The theory of imperialism developed by J.A. Schumpeter, which sees it as an atavistic survival of the aggression and lust for conquest of primitive warrior states, exemplifies one of the problems with this approach by obscuring the connection between modern economic structures and modern imperialism.[15] Another is the pseudo-Darwinian idea that aggression and the drive to maximise reproductive opportunities, resulting in empire, are universal traits of human behaviour and hence can never be changed.[16] However, the solution is not to restrict the term 'imperialism' to a specific and strictly modern phenomenon, but rather to strike a balance between sameness and difference, with regard both to the variations between different historical imperialisms and to the contexts within which they developed. Lenin's account of imperialism, for all its indebtedness to Bukharin, offers a more moderate line in this regard:

> Colonial policy and imperialism existed before this latest stage of capitalism, and even before capitalism. Rome, founded on slavery, pursued a colonial policy and practised imperialism.

But 'general' disquisitions on imperialism, which ignore, or put into the background, the fundamental difference between social-economic systems, inevitably degenerate into the most vapid banality or bragging, like the comparison 'Greater Rome and Greater Britain'.[17]

Similarly, understanding the overall process of Roman expansion is a matter of balancing generalisations with specifics: drawing on modern theories as a source of ideas about how societies work and therefore how the ancient evidence might (rather than must) be interpreted, and modifying the understanding of 'imperialism' as a more general historical phenomenon in the light of the Roman experience.

The study of Roman imperialism seeks to identify patterns and consistencies in the mass of detail and individual events, and to evaluate their significance. Inevitably it involves questions of how far, and in what respect, a particular episode might be seen as typical or representative. The events of the Third Punic War, for example, fit very poorly with the idea that Roman imperialism was defensive, but they are also difficult to reconcile with any theory that sees Roman expansion as fully rational; on the contrary, the main motive (epitomised by Cato's fig-dropping performance) appears to be an entirely irrational fear and hatred of the old enemy Carthage, even after it had been thoroughly defeated and stripped of any significant power. The episode might, then, be seen as an aberration (and the choice of it as the opening example for this chapter regarded as tendentious, designed to present the Roman Empire in the worst possible light); alternatively it might be claimed, by a theory of imperialism such as Schumpeter's, as a perfect example of the behaviour of ancient states, even if their aggressive instincts were normally better concealed behind pretexts and claims to be acting justly.

Neither of these positions is entirely convincing. Rome's past history of bitter conflict with Carthage, and above all the legacy of Hannibal's invasion of Italy, meant that this was in some respects a special case; however, it was not entirely *sui generis*, and any theory of Roman imperialism needs to be able to account for this war as well as other, more straightforward episodes. Three points are particularly worth noting. The first is the complexity of decision-making in Rome, and hence the difficulty for modern historians in divining the motives behind decisions. A straightforward narrative of events in which 'the senate decided' or 'the Romans resolved' conceals the extent to which there was debate, perhaps serious debate, about the decision to undertake any particular war, and about whether or not to annex a particular territory after victory. In the case of the final war on Carthage we find an apparent conflict between the assertions of Greek historians like Polybius and Appian that 'the senate' had long since resolved to make war on Carthage and was simply waiting for a pretext, and the account of Cato's role in obsessively promoting an anti-Carthaginian policy at every opportunity. At the very least there seems to be a disagreement about timing and tactics – Polybius suggested that 'their disputes with each other about the effect on foreign opinion very nearly made them desist from going to war' (36.2) – but perhaps there was disagreement about more fundamental matters of strategy. The issue of Roman motivation is complicated further by the complexity of its political system, with different elements having different powers and remits, each being able on occasion to press the others into supporting their wishes:

> Now the elements by which the Roman constitution was controlled were three in number, all of which I have mentioned before, and all the aspects of the administration were, taken separately, so fairly and so suitably ordered and regulated through the agency of these three elements that it was impossible even for the Romans themselves to declare with certainty whether the whole system was an aristocracy, a democracy or a monarchy. In fact it was quite natural that this should be so, for if we were to fix our eyes only on the power of the consuls, the constitution might give the impression of being completely monarchical and royal; if we confined our attention to the senate it would seem to be aristocratic; and if we looked at the power of the people it would appear to be a clear example of a democracy.
>
> (Polybius, *Histories*, 6.11.11–12)

It should be noted further that while 'the senate' (or 'the Roman elite') can often be thought of as a unified bloc dedicated to the maintenance of its own power and interests against the mass of the population, it was in practice riven with factions and rivalries. Insofar as the senate showing any signs of coherent organisation, rather than simply being a collection of individuals focused on their own interests, the dividing lines were between ill-defined groups connected by ties of kinship, friendship or advantage, not between parties united around beliefs or political programmes. The study of Roman imperialism is not the study of the explicit and univocal policy of a government or ruler, or of their concealed but fully conscious ambitions, but of the structures that shaped the decisions taken by the individuals in the senate, the magistrates and the people of Rome over the course of centuries. The cumulative result is clear enough, but it is entirely plausible that it developed from a combination of different motives and interests, irrational as well as rational, and that the eloquence of an individual speaker might at times be as significant in determining the course of events as the interests of a larger group. Under the Principate, the decision-making process became simpler, resting on the judgement or whim of an individual emperor under the influence of different advisors – and it is striking that there is significantly less disagreement amongst historians about the nature of Roman rule over the Empire than about the process by which the bulk of the Empire was acquired.

The second significant point is the possibility that Roman imperialism changed over time, and not simply with the end of large-scale expansionism under Augustus. Certainly the Third Punic War was interpreted by some contemporary Greeks as representing a change in approach; Polybius reports them as 'saying that far from maintaining the principles by which they [the Romans] had won their supremacy, they were little by little deserting it for a lust of domination like that of Athens and Sparta' (37.1). Some Roman authors, looking back from the political disorder of the first century BCE, saw the war as the moment when they had lost the favour of the gods by acting unjustly. In more material terms, the success of Roman imperialism changed the conditions under which future wars took place. Their armies came to operate over increasingly large areas and different sorts of terrain, creating new problems of logistics, communication and the supervision of generals; they encountered new kinds of opponents, from the city states of southern Italy, Sicily and Greece to the empires of Carthage and Macedon, and the disordered tribes of Spain, Gaul and Germany. At the same time Rome itself changed, and thus the context of decision-making: the influx of wealth altered the workings of the political system and the balance between its different components, while the relationship between Rome and her allies, and between the citizen population and the army, were affected by dramatic changes in the economy and society of Italy as it became the centre of a Mediterranean-wide empire.[18] There were sufficient continuities in the structures that shaped Roman imperialism to continue to think of it as a single phenomenon, as will be discussed below, but it was never entirely uniform.

The third point relates to our sources. It is not simply that, as in the history of many other empires, we have to rely primarily on the accounts of the imperialists themselves with scarcely anything from the perspective of the conquered and colonised; in the case of the Roman Empire we have a significant number of important accounts from Greek writers, who reached an accommodation with Rome early on but nevertheless do offer an alternative perspective.[19] Rather, it is the fact that most accounts of the growth of Roman power were written in retrospect, from the perspective of the crises of the last century of the Republic or from the vantage point of the new monarchical order established after the civil wars by Augustus. Roman histories of their Empire are not simply or invariably self-serving and justificatory – indeed, they offer some remarkable denunciations of Roman imperialism that have been quoted by opponents of empire ever since – but they do naturally interpret the past according to present concerns and in the service of present needs. Sallust's account of Roman imperialism before and after the defeat of Carthage, written around 42 BCE, offers an example:

> And so the power of the republic increased through diligence and justice. Powerful kings were vanquished, savage tribes and huge nations were brought down; and when Carthage, Rome's imperial rival, had been destroyed, every land and sea lay open to Rome. It was then that fortune turned unkind and confounded all of Rome's enterprises. To the men who had so easily endured toil and peril, anxiety and adversity, the leisure and riches which are generally regarded as so desirable proved a burden and a curse. Growing avarice, and the lust for power which followed it, gave birth to every kind of evil. Avarice destroyed honour, integrity and every other virtue, and instead taught men to be proud and cruel, to neglect religion and to hold nothing too sacred to sell.
>
> (Sallust, *The War Against Catiline*, 10)

Clearly this cannot be taken at face value. First-century accounts, both of the past and of contemporary imperialism, were fully implicated in the struggle for power and the control of meaning as the republic tottered; Caesar's reports back to Rome of his own activities in Gaul are simply the most extreme example. Later histories, written under the stultifying influence of powerful and temperamental monarchs, were similarly influenced or distorted. To uncover the reality of Roman imperialism, it is necessary to confront not only the way that Rome was mythologised by later societies but also the myths and polemics that the Romans developed themselves.

MOTIVATION AND IDEOLOGY

One approach to understanding Roman imperialism is to focus on the factors that inclined the Romans to make war: not the specific tactical or political considerations that affected an individual decision, but the general conceptions and ideological structures that made it more likely than not, especially under the Middle Republic (up to the mid second century BCE), that Rome would despatch an army in any given year. As discussed above, the nature of the decision-making process in Rome means that the reasons behind any individual decision were almost certainly mixed, but, at least for the elite, it is possible to identify a number of consistent factors shaping their choices.[20]

The first was an obsessive concern for security. It is not necessary to accept the Romans' claims that all (or nearly all) their wars were fought in self-defence to recognise that these claims were not simply a sop to public opinion, whether in Rome (where the people might be reluctant to fight except in defence of their home) or across the Mediterranean (where trust in Rome's good faith could be as important as fear of Roman power in keeping allies and neutrals in line). The early years of Roman history established a mindset of prickly defensiveness and suspicion: the fifth century had been a desperate struggle to resist the attacks of powerful neighbours; the beginning of the fourth century saw Celtic raids into Italy and the sack of Rome itself around 386 BCE; and the third century brought Pyrrhus of Epirus and a mercenary army, invited across from Greece by the city of Tarentum to check Roman power, and then the Carthaginians. The Romans had a strong sense of their own past, kept alive by handing down stories of their heroic ancestors (and, according to some historians, through the regular performance of historical plays) long before they began to write formal history.[21] They internalised not only the values of the past but also its sense of being surrounded by a hostile world; and, of course, as their success in repelling one enemy brought them increased power and wealth and thus persuaded others of the need to check their growing power, the world frequently confirmed their suspicions.[22] Any city or nation that was not under firm Roman control, whether informal or formal, was a potential threat, if not in itself then because it might ally with a rival power. Rome did become less belligerent (at least in terms of the number of wars) after the Second Punic War because it no longer faced an enemy that could menace its own existence; but, as the final destruction of Carthage shows, the senate could still be persuaded to act aggressively in the supposed interests of Roman security.

One element in Roman decision-making, therefore, was a genuine – if sometimes entirely groundless – fear of the consequences if they failed to intervene in a region perceived as troublesome. However, the fact that we hear about Roman generals being criticised for suspected war-mongering makes it clear that there were other factors which made war seem an attractive as well as necessary policy to members of the elite. The most obvious was gain.[23] Successful war-making and conquest were generally profitable for all concerned: slaves and booty were seized in the immediate aftermath of victory (the defeat of Macedon in 167 BCE brought in 120 million sesterces of booty); countries that were allowed to remain independent might be required to pay large indemnities to Rome, while those that were annexed as provinces had to pay regular tribute in cash or goods (Macedonia yielded an annual revenue of 2.4 million sesterces). Large areas of land could be confiscated and redistributed to Roman settlers and members of the elite, while assets like mines and quarries were taken into Roman ownership (the Spanish silver mines produced 36.5 million sesterces every year). These profits were spread throughout Roman society: not only amongst the victorious general and his troops, the rapacious governor and the societies of tax-collectors, but Roman society as a whole, with large-scale building projects and distributions of grain funded from the proceeds of conquest. Of course, not all conquests were equally profitable or could compare with the enormous riches captured from the empires of the East; if a strict cost–benefit analysis were applied, it is highly arguable whether the efforts to conquer and subdue some regions were really worth it (the income from the Spanish silver mines, for example, barely covered the costs of pacifying the region).[24] But the Romans did not apply cost–benefit analyses in a consistent manner: the military resources were available, in the form of the duty of citizens to serve in the army and the requirement on Rome's Italian allies to supply troops, so that one might almost speak of an opportunity cost if these forces were not employed productively in war in a given year.[25] The expedition into Dalmatia in 156 BCE, on the grounds that the army needed exercise, was an extreme example (there had also been raids across the frontier and insults as provocation), but it is revealing of the Romans' casual attitude towards the deployment of their forces when they were not confronted with a really serious threat.[26] The costs and benefits of making war were not equally shared, so that the consuls had little reason to hesitate even if a majority in the senate was reluctant to take on further commitments; further, reliable information was inevitably in short supply, so that rumours of a country's wealth might be sufficient to persuade waverers. This is not to say that all, or even any, decisions to go to war were made solely for reasons of profit, but they were always made with an awareness of the likely profitability of conquest for those involved.

Discussion of the material motivation for Roman war-making sometimes becomes conflated with modern ideas of 'economic imperialism', in which overseas interventions are seen to be driven by national economic interests or by special interest groups lobbying and bribing the decision-makers. There is little evidence to suggest that this was a significant factor in antiquity.[27] The Romans did not conceptualise 'the economy' as a significant sector of society, and certainly did not regard it as part of the role of the state to promote trade or economic growth.[28] On a few occasions the stated grounds for military intervention were to protect Roman or Italian traders from harassment by pirates (for example, in Illyria in 229 BCE; Polybius, 2.8.3), but this seems to be a matter of defending citizens as a matter of national pride and status, and of responding to a threat to Roman security and dominance, rather than protecting trade per se. The *publicani*, the groups of businessmen who bought up contracts to supply the army, collect tribute and manage state assets, are known on occasion to have lobbied the senate in favour of military action, but the chief example is their call for Macedonia to be annexed in 167 BCE to gain control of its mines, a call which was ignored.[29] It is possible that other, more successful attempts at persuasion may have remained unrecorded, but it is important to remember that any such attempt had to win over not a leader or a party but a large number of individual senators. In practical terms, it was impossible to persuade the senate to agree to a policy that a majority of its members did not believe was in their own best interests.

From the perspective of the individual member of the Roman elite, financial profit was not the only possible gain from successful military action; there was also glory.[30] Young aristocratic men were inculcated with an ideology of public service, encouraged to devote their lives to outdoing both their contemporaries and their predecessors. In the words that Cicero placed in the mouth of Scipio Africanus, 'all those who have preserved, aided or enlarged their fatherland have a special place prepared for them in the heavens' (*Republic*, 6.13).

> As soon as the young men could endure the hardships of war, they were taught a soldier's duties in camp under a vigorous discipline, and they took more pleasure in handsome arms and war horses than in harlots and revelry. To such men consequently no labour was unfamiliar, no region too rough or too steep, no armed enemy was terrible; courage was everything. Their hardest struggle was with each other; each man strove to be the first to strike down the foe, to scale a wall, to be seen by all while doing such a deed. This they considered virtue, this fair fame and high nobility.
>
> (Sallust, *The War Against Catiline*, 7.4–6)

Sallust's account of the virtuous Republic of the past is driven by the contrast with the 'decadent' Republic of his own time, dominated in his opinion by avarice and luxury; it may not be historically accurate, therefore, but it does clearly express the ideals of the Roman elite, the values which they *believed* should determine their behaviour. The Roman noble was trained in warfare and in military values from an early age; his public career began as a military tribune and, as he proceeded through the *cursus honorum*, the ladder of official positions, his terms of office as a magistrate and a member of the senate were interspersed with further periods of military service. War provided opportunities for glory, and a basis for the greater glory of attaining the higher magistracies; an impressive war record was one of the most important qualities that an aristocrat could display to persuade the people to vote for his candidacy. In turn, the consulship entailed command of an army and the possibility – if Rome went to war – of gaining the highest honour of a triumph. Such glory was not essential for political success – by the second century, at any rate, the example of Cato shows that it was possible to build a career on the basis of civilian attributes like oratory – but it remained central to Roman ideology even after the system of competition for office had collapsed. A weak emperor like Claudius, dependent on the continuing support of the military, would make war in order to establish his credentials as the head of the Roman Empire and the army's commander in chief. Other emperors sought to match or out-do their predecessors and, just as importantly, to limit the opportunities for potential rivals to win glory by permitting only members of the imperial clan to celebrate triumphs.[31]

This militarised value system and atmosphere of fierce competition for honour and status would clearly prompt any consul to adopt a bellicose attitude during his term of office, seeking to make the best advantage of the single year in which he had command of an army (while perhaps picking and choosing possible theatres of operations; there was always more prestige in bringing a war to a close than in starting one for a rival to conclude). The fact that military achievements clearly did carry weight with voters implies that the people shared the elite view that the best leaders were the most successful generals. There is almost no direct evidence for the attitudes of the masses towards war, except that Rome experienced little difficulty in recruiting troops for most of its wars before the second century. It was a taken-for-granted duty of a Roman citizen to serve in the militia; Roman society (including the way that citizens were organised into groups for voting) was structured like a military camp, and so we might imagine that the ideology of war as normal and praiseworthy was pervasive. The senate was the obvious arena for more mixed opinions: on the one hand, senators might be reluctant to grant a rival the opportunity for glory; on the other, they had the same unquestioning belief in the virtues of military activity and a concern for the reputation of Rome itself – the favour of the gods might depend on maintaining faith with one's allies, even those acquired only recently for solely tactical purposes, while every victory added to the prestige and standing of Rome even more than it did to that of the individual general.

INTERNATIONAL RELATIONS

The focus on motivation and the ideology that underpinned it suggests reasons why the Romans were generally inclined to make war on their neighbours, while the need to balance different ends – to prevent an individual's drive for glory and profit from compromising Rome's security, for example – and, above all, the complex decision-making process show why their policy was never wholly consistent. However, this 'psychological' approach to understanding imperialism has a number of problems and limitations. It takes the Romans' mindset and ideology entirely for granted – an assumption not too far removed from Schumpeter's belief in the universality of innate primitive aggression – rather than considering the possibility that a militarised ideology might be the product rather than the cause of a tradition of violent relations with the rest of the world. Furthermore, this approach focuses solely on decisions taken at the centre; imperialism is seen as a directed, conscious process in which the conquering power imposes itself on other nations. Essentially, however far it expresses or implies criticism of their actions, this 'metrocentric' approach adopts wholesale the perspective of the conqueror and coloniser.[32]

Some recent studies of modern imperialism have therefore sought to focus instead on the imperial periphery, the regions outside the empire.[33] The aim is to understand the conditions that make a country vulnerable to external interference, whether or not that results in formal annexation (this approach can also be productive in understanding the fate of regions in the post-colonial era, precisely because it focuses on the state of 'native society' rather than on the aims and actions of the conquerors).[34] Applied to the Roman period, a focus on the periphery emphasises the wide variety of situations faced by the Romans in the course of their expansion – from established empires such as Carthage and Egypt; to the mosaic of small, disunited statelets in Greece; to the pre-state, tribal societies of Spain and Gaul.[35] It was not just that these polities had to be handled in different ways and represented different levels of threat; in many cases, conditions at the periphery created opportunities for Rome to intervene, or left them with little choice but to get involved. Rivalries amongst the Greek states and their fear of Macedon led them to seek the protection of an alliance with a greater power; the Romans sought to protect their interests through strategic alliances with neighbouring states, but could then find themselves pulled into local affairs, or in conflict with another of the major powers, as a result.

The same happened in Gaul in the first century BCE when one tribe, the Helvetii, sought to pass through the territory of another tribe that had long-standing ties with the Romans and who called on them for help (Caesar, *Gallic War*, 1.11). Of course, the Romans might in theory refuse a request for assistance, but that would damage their credibility with other allies and create an impression of weakness in the face of potential enemies. Having seen off the Helvetii, Caesar was then approached by representatives of a confederation of Gallic tribes and asked to intervene against the German Ariovistus who had established dominion over an area of eastern Gaul.

The most important consideration was the fact that the Aedui, who had frequently been styled by the senate 'Brothers and Kinsmen of the Roman People' were enslaved and held subject by the Germans, and that Aeduan hostages were in the hands of Ariovistus and the Sequani, which, considering the mighty power of Rome, Caesar regarded as a disgrace to himself and his country. Furthermore, if the Germans gradually formed a habit of crossing the Rhine and entering Gaul in large numbers, he saw how dangerous it would be for the Romans... Moreover, Ariovistus personally had behaved with quite intolerable arrogance and pride.

(*Gallic War*, 1.33)

The result was the extension of Roman dominance over a large area of Gaul, provoking the northern tribes into gathering their forces and thus providing grounds for further war and conquest. It is an important reminder that, while some groups on the periphery actively invited Roman intervention, and the disordered or disunited state of some peripheral societies made them ripe for conquest, the Romans were rarely slow to recognise the material benefits of maintaining Rome's reputation for aiding its allies. Recognition that conquered nations and peoples were not always wholly passive victims of Roman aggression can too easily shade into a new version of the 'defensive imperialism' thesis, an apology for imperialism. Empire comes to be justified as the source of order in an anarchic world, saving weak and inferior societies from themselves: 'the growth of Roman dominion was the necessary and natural advance of a genuine governing nation in a world politically disordered, like the advance of the English in India'.[36] Similar rhetoric has been brought forward in recent decades to support an interventionist United States foreign policy, presented as a response to calls for assistance and liberation from smaller nations oppressed by their neighbours or rulers, and as the means of establishing the necessary conditions of peace and security for the benign processes of globalization.[37]

An alternative approach seeks to interpret imperialism in terms of the doctrines of the realist school of international relations theory.[38] States, it is assumed, seek always to maximise their power as a means of self-preservation in the face of other power-maximising states within an anarchic and highly competitive world. War is ubiquitous as the normal means of resolving conflicts of interest between states, and a state which is successful in war naturally seeks to take full advantage of this to bolster its position. Empire, therefore, is simply the natural result of a state adapting especially well to its hostile environment, or possessing some material advantage over its rivals. The ancient Mediterranean was undoubtedly anarchic, with no international law, poor and slow communications and no means of enforcing the few rules of conduct between states besides fear of the gods; war was indeed ubiquitous, and it is clear that Rome's militaristic culture was shaped by this environment – as were the cultures of many other states. As discussed above, it is clear that concerns for security and fear of a rival gaining advantage were crucial influences on the decision of both Carthage and Rome to intervene in Sicily in 264 BCE, and other episodes, especially Rome's interactions with the empires of Macedon and Syria in the East, can be interpreted similarly. However, the conception of state motivation in realist theory is unhelpfully narrow, ignoring the complexity of the decision-making process and the significance of different interests and interest groups even in the modern world, let alone in Rome.[39] The theory tends to take for granted the existence of modern nation-states as the actors in international relations, whereas the 'states' of classical antiquity were more loosely structured and far more disparate in nature, and hence inclined to follow different strategies for power maximisation – to say nothing of those areas which had at best proto-state structures. In important respects, Rome's environment was more anarchic, complex and unpredictable than that assumed by realist theory, so that its assumptions about the nature of relations between power-maximising, security-obsessed states offer at best only a partial, and very general, guide to the dynamics of Roman imperialism.

THE RISE AND FALL OF THE MILITARY–POLITICAL–AGRICULTURAL COMPLEX

The international relations approach, whatever its questionable aspects, places an important emphasis on the role of systems and constraints in determining the course of historical events. Roman imperialists were never in the position of making entirely free decisions; their choices were always conditioned, partly by external circumstances and partly by the workings of their own society. Whether or not this was entirely a response to the hostility of their environment, war was internalised to the extent of being not merely an expectation and an ideal for Rome's elite but a requirement for the proper functioning of society. There were two different, interdependent processes in Rome which drove the acquisition of empire and the defeat of all significant external threats. In due course, as a result of their very success, they also became a source of disruption and social breakdown, bringing about the collapse of the Roman political system, its refoundation as an autocracy and significant changes in external behaviour, as the price of retaining the Empire.

The first process has already been mentioned: the cycle of accumulation of the Roman elite.[40] The ultimate goal was family power and prestige: material resources were accumulated as a means of gaining status and, especially, of gaining the opportunity for military glory by holding political office; political and military power were used as a means of accumulating material resources. There was no logical end to the cycle, no point at which a family or individual might conclude that they had amassed sufficient wealth and honours, only an incessant comparison with the successes of other families and individuals in accumulation. However, the success of Roman imperialism and the stability of Roman society, which created these opportunities for elite aggrandisement, depended on ensuring a balance between competition and solidarity, and thus on imposing a certain number of rules on the contest. The great fear was that one individual might gain an excess of power and seek to take over the game altogether, so the system incorporated a range of checks: the short duration of magistracies; limits on the number of terms; set periods between one magistracy and the next; the principle of collegiality, so that the actions of every magistrate were subject to the veto of a colleague with equal powers and status; laws to try to control the scale of resources that could be expended in competition for office; and the informal sanctions at the disposal of the senate, such as threatening to withhold honours from successful generals if they over-stepped the boundaries. The system sought to ensure that individual and state interests reinforced one another to the benefit of both; it encouraged fierce competition, in the service of the power of Rome as a whole, not least through the way that the most able were forced to exert themselves ever harder as they climbed up the *cursus honorum*. Every year, 20 *quaestors* (the lowest level of magistrate) were elected; in due course, the survivors of those 20 would be competing with one another, and with older senators, for just two consulships.[41]

The cycle of elite accumulation drove Rome's tendency to make war; however, it would never have endured or even come into existence without the support of a second process that made Rome's sustained military activities possible.[42] This process operated within

Roman and Italian society as a whole, and might be termed a cycle of sustainability; its effect was that war became embedded in the economy and society. For centuries Roman wars were fought with citizen militias, both Roman citizens and the troops supplied by the allies, founded on the sort of peasant patriarch whose image dominated later Roman literature as the essence of true Romanness, fighting for the most part during the quiet agricultural season. War served as a means for the profit of the elite without alienating the masses; taxes were kept low, partly because the state provided only very limited services and partly because the system was organised around military service as an alternative means of surplus appropriation.[43] The peasants benefited both directly (from booty) and indirectly (from low taxes and public amenities) as a result of successful conquest; war could therefore be used as a distraction and an outlet for the energies of the masses, which might otherwise have been directed against the dominance of the elite – certainly this was how some ancient sources presented it. Even when military service became more arduous with the expansion of the Empire, because of year-round garrison duties, long wars and distant overseas commitments, it remained manageable because of the way that the life-cycle of the peasant family worked; a farm could cope with the absence of a son for a period of years, and benefited, or at least was compensated, from the additional income from wages and booty.

For the individual household, of course, it was a serious problem if their son was killed or crippled, especially if he was the only heir. As far as Italian society as a whole was concerned, however, the effort was sustainable; Italy benefited from the influx of revenue as well as from the 'demographic sink' effect because war casualties kept population growth low, and thus ensured that living standards were maintained, or possibly even improved, without any increase in productivity. However, this meant that regular wars became a necessity; without the flow of tribute and the draining of excess manpower, the Italian population might have risen relative to the available resources, leading to widespread impoverishment and the possibility of rebellion against those who controlled the lion's share of social wealth. That is not to say that the Roman elite perceived the situation in these terms or were conscious of its underlying dynamic; they simply took advantage of the willingness of their citizens to fight and the availability of troops from their Italian allies. Behind the scenes, Italian society had become geared to regular war, both culturally and economically; Rome rarely had problems in finding soldiers for its conflicts, even in the periods of more or less constant war up to the second century, so there was no constraint on the drive to accumulation of the elite.[44]

For centuries, Roman imperial expansion was driven by the interaction and reciprocal reinforcement of these two cycles. By the middle of the second century, however, problems were beginning to emerge, largely as a result of the system's success. The conquest of the wealthy east, above all, brought about a dramatic increase in the profits to be made from political offices; so did the competition for them, and so too the amount of expenditure now required to have a reasonable chance of getting elected. Family resources were often no longer sufficient; Roman notables began to speculate on the potential rewards of office, and their willingness to spend heavily on gaining supporters and bribing the electorate then created the necessity for them either to launch a grand military campaign or to despoil their province in order to pay off the debts they had accumulated. It is clear that many senators chose to opt out of this increasingly uncontrolled competition, content to reach the lowest tier of the *cursus honorum* and to concentrate on accumulation through exploitation of existing resources rather than active dispossession. However, a small number of individuals whose speculations in power had paid off became ever more powerful, able to dictate to the senate, demand the ratification of their actions even if technically illegal (for example, Pompey's conquests in the East and the administrative arrangements he put in place without any consultation) and lead armies against other Roman citizens. Each of these men was fearful of the power of the others, alternating between uneasy alliances with one another against the attempts of members of the senate to place restrictions on their power (the obvious example is the 'first triumvirate', the pact between Caesar, Pompey and Crassus in 60 BCE) and seeking to counter one another's ambitions. Both Pompey and Caesar became immensely wealthy as the result of their conquests, but it was impossible for them to leave the competition and give up their armies for fear of losing everything if prosecuted by their enemies. The interests of the state were now firmly subordinated to those of a few powerful individuals, driven to establish their position through military endeavour – but those individuals were equally trapped in the dynamics of the cycle of conquest.

Meanwhile, imperial success brought about far-reaching changes in the economy of Italy, with the growth of the city of Rome and other major urban centres and the establishment of slave-run, market-orientated villas in central Italy.[45] New economic opportunities appeared, subsidised by the proceeds of empire, but peasant families whose sons were overseas – or who had been killed in battle – were less able to take advantage of them or to afford the investment that would take them to a higher level of prosperity.[46] Furthermore, there was now fierce competition for the most fertile and well-situated land, as members of the land-owning elite sought to respond to the new market opportunities by taking a more rational approach to agricultural production. In areas of central Italy, peasant farms were increasingly put under pressure; not destroyed, as is clear from the archaeological record, but pushed towards the margins and disconnected from the networks of markets.[47] Increasingly, families falling into difficulty through debt or illness preferred to move to the city, imagining the golden opportunities that might be found there; to keep this ever-growing urban population quiet and avoid giving further opportunities to populist politicians, the state needed to use its revenue to subsidise the city food supply and provide public services – which attracted further migrants. Faced with an apparent crisis in the peasantry, the traditional source of soldiers, the state began to recruit from the *capite censi*, those counted by head in the census because they failed to meet the lowest wealth qualification. The result was an increasingly professionalised army, but one loyal to its commanders rather than to the state because it was the general who depended on his troops for power and security, who took responsibility for compelling the senate to allocate land for veteran settlement and thus provided security for retired soldiers. Such armies were powerful tools in the hands of individual generals, but at the same time they placed their commanders in the position of having to fight further wars in order to maintain their position.

Rome continued to make war because it had no choice; the alternative seemed to be the collapse of the political system and the revolutionary redistribution of the rewards of empire in a way that was unacceptable to those who held power, even though the stability of society was being undermined by the very processes that had sustained and driven Roman imperialism. The result, after a series of civil wars between the remaining dynasts, was twofold: the replacement of the republican system with a monarchy, albeit one which retained many of the old forms and titles and professed itself to be a restoration of the republic, and the end of the cycle of conquests.[48] The trend towards exploitation rather than violent appropriation had been developing for some time, but the advent of the Principate accelerated the process. Social stability now required the steady stream of revenue that could be gained from exploiting existing provinces rather than seizing new ones; Italy was no longer a reliable source of military recruits, whereas the provinces were beginning to reveal their potential as a source of manpower. Emperors were no longer competing directly with anyone (except their predecessors and the idealised image of the good emperor) and were more concerned to limit the possibility of anyone else gaining glory than to win it themselves. The emperor effectively became the state (not least through a stupendous effort of image creation and propaganda under Augustus), so that the loyalty of the army was, generally, focused on his person and thus subordinated to the interests of the Empire. Above all, the emperor's claim to legitimacy was that he brought peace to the Empire, and breaking what had become a destructive relationship between wealth, power and war was a prerequisite for that. Of course, the Roman conception of 'peace' did not necessarily accord with that of their subjects.

2
'They Make a Desert and Call it Peace': The Nature of Roman Rule

Robbers of the world, now that the earth is insufficient for their all-devastating hands they probe even the sea; if their enemy is rich, they are greedy; if he is poor, they thirst for dominion; neither east nor west has satisfied them; alone of mankind they are equally covetous of poverty and wealth. Robbery, slaughter and plunder they falsely name empire; they make a desert and they call it peace.

(Tacitus, *Agricola*, 30.4)

Different interpretations of the dynamics of Roman conquest have been deployed to legitimise modern empire-building as just, defensive or accidental, and just as often cited in condemnations of overseas aggression or gunboat diplomacy.[1] However, with the exception of Fascist propaganda presenting Roman domination of the Mediterranean as the template and justification for a new Italian imperialism, and Hitler's avowed admiration for their aggression ('In every peace treaty, the next war is already built in. That is Rome! That is true statesmanship!'), Roman conquests were not proposed or taken as models for actual modern practice.[2] The manner in which the Roman Empire was ruled was a quite different matter; indeed, Roman conquests were frequently excused as the necessary means to the establishment of peace and civilisation across Europe, and modern imperialism justified because it created the possibility of equalling Rome's achievement as a ruler of other nations in other regions of the world. Rome's exemplary status as an empire was based above all on its longevity and the absence of serious internal opposition or conflict, and this was attributed to its benevolent and beneficent impact on the areas it had conquered.[3] As the English historian J.R. Seeley put it, 'Imperialism, introducing system and unity, gave the Roman world in the first place internal tranquillity.'[4]

This theme was especially popular in nineteenth- and early twentieth-century British commentaries on empire: 'its imperial system, alike in its differences and similarities, lights up our own Empire, for example in India, at every turn'.[5] The example was not taken as universally relevant; in contrast to the British Dominions, the Romans

had not succeeded in raising their subjects to point of self-govern-
ment, not least because their empire had focused on the conquest
and rule of already-occupied regions rather than the settlement
of (supposedly) uninhabited areas. 'They gave organization, laws,
institutions, language, roads and buildings, but they did not give
birth to and rear from subordination to equality young peoples of
their own Roman race.'[6] In India, and later Africa, however, the
British confronted the same problem of ruling an uncivilised foreign
population, and could hope to learn from Rome's achievements.
As Charles Trevelyan suggested in 1838, 'acquisitions made by
superiority in war were consolidated by superiority in peace; and the
remembrance of the original violence was lost in that of the benefits
which resulted from it... The Indians will, I hope, soon stand in
the same position towards us in which we once stood towards the
Romans.'[7] Roman imperialism was justified by its results, and the
British could hope for the same, although for the moment, with
regard to their policy towards the natives, 'British Imperialism has,
in so far as the indigenous races of Asia and Africa are concerned,
been a failure.'[8] After all, the imperial rulers shared the same ideals:

> The success of the British, like that of the Roman administra-
> tion in securing peace and good order, has been due, not merely
> to a sense of the interest every government has in maintaining
> conditions which, because favourable to industry are favourable
> also to revenue, but also to the high ideal of the duties of a rule
> which both nations have set before themselves.[9]

These references to Roman rule constantly return to three crucial
points: the establishment of order and peace, the integration of the
conquered natives into the system, and the bringing of civilisation
to primitive regions. For a number of these writers, the first of
these is demonstrably the most important, both as the basis for
future development and as an alibi for the undeniable disruption
and destruction of conquest:

> Those who watch India most impartially see that a vast trans-
> formation goes on there, but sometimes it produces a painful
> impression upon them; they see much destroyed, bad things
> and good things together; sometimes they doubt whether they
> see many good things called into existence. But they see one
> enormous improvement, under which we may fairly hope that
> all other improvements are potentially included, they see anarchy

and plunder brought to an end and something like the *immensa majestas Romanae pacis* [the immense majesty of the Roman peace] established among two hundred and fifty millions of human beings.[10]

It is striking that even works which made use of Roman examples in order to attack British imperialism, such as J.M. Robertson's *Patriotism and Empire*, failed to engage with the positive evaluation of Roman rule and its impact on the conquered territories under the Principate, but focused instead on the rapaciousness of the Republican conquerors and the role of empire in the decay of liberty in Rome itself.[11] The establishment of order and civilisation across the empire is clearly not regarded as sufficient justification for imperialism – but its achievement does not appear to be disputed.

Modern studies of imperialism make some remarkably similar assumptions about the Roman Empire, offering a sharp contrast between the process of its acquisition and the system of imperial rule, and focusing on the success of the latter, demonstrated by its longevity. Michael Mann's study of social power characterises this as the shift from an empire of domination to a territorial empire, emphasising that Rome 'was one of the most successful conquering states in all history, but it was *the* most successful *retainer* of conquests'.[12] Michael Doyle, meanwhile, coined the concept of the 'Augustan threshold' for the shift from violent conquest to benign and sustainable rule, and applied this idea more widely as an explanation for the failures of the Spanish and the first English overseas empires: 'The root cause of the collapse of the English empire in America was England's failure to cross the Augustan Threshold.'[13] Both stress the importance of stability and order, and, above all, the integration of local elites into the imperial state for Rome's achievement.

These ideas are echoed in more popular contemporary discussions; indeed, it is clear that they underpin most of the arguments that present 'empire', in the form of United States hegemony, as a desirable global future. Deepak Lal's account talks in general terms of the role played by empires in quelling international anarchy and offering 'the essential public good of order', bureaucracy, law, market prices and predictable human relations over a wide area, all at a reasonable cost; the only example cited, besides the United States as a potential imperial power, is Rome.[14] Other writers are prepared to allow a positive case for Britain as well:

Throughout history, peace and stability have been a major benefit of empires. In fact, *pax romana* in Latin means the Roman peace, or the stability brought about by the Roman Empire. Rome's power was so overwhelming that no one could challenge it successfully for hundreds of years. The result was stability within the Roman Empire. Where Rome conquered, peace, law, order, education, a common language, and much else followed. That was true of the British Empire (*pax Britannica*) too. So it is with the United States today.[15]

This impression of the essential benevolence and positive consequences of Roman rule is deep-seated; opponents of modern imperialism generally question its appropriateness for a contemporary context rather than dispute its historical accuracy. And yet the Roman sources themselves raised questions about whether the empire's longevity was due to its enlightened administration rather than to the efficiency of its systems of control and coercion: examples include the words which Tacitus put into the mouth of the (otherwise unknown) British chieftain Calgacus at the end of the first century CE, quoted at the beginning of this chapter, or the unselfconscious menace in the account of his achievements left by the emperor who gave his name to the 'Augustan threshold': 'When foreign peoples could safely be pardoned, I preferred to preserve rather than to exterminate them' (Augustus, *Res Gestae*, 3.2).

PACIFICATION

In the Republican period, Roman accounts exhibited few illusions about the level of resistance to their rule and the necessity of continued force to subdue most of the regions they controlled, for a considerable time after conquest. In relatively 'civilised' areas with well-established city-state systems, such as Greece and Asia Minor, the main concern was that individual cities might seek to change sides or revolt when Rome was threatened by an enemy like the Macedonians or Parthians. When he represented the people and cities of Sicily in court against their former governor Verres, Cicero took great pains to insist on the province's long-standing loyalty to Rome, and still could not conceal the fact that this loyalty had never been complete or unquestioning: 'once the various states in the island had embraced our friendship, they never thereafter seceded from it; and most of them, and those the most notable, remained our firm friends without interruption' (*Against Verres*, II.2.2). At the other end of the spectrum, in a region like Gaul, there was constant attritional warfare against different tribal groups; Caesar spent almost all of his time there dealing with a succession of revolts against Roman power, and in less than ten years was said to have seized 800 settlements and sold over 1 million captives into slavery (Plutarch, *Caesar*, 15.5). Many provinces offered a mixture of the two situations: untrustworthy and opportunistic 'allies', and defiant opponents. Arriving in Cilicia in 51 BCE as its new governor amid rumours that a large Parthian force had crossed the Euphrates and was menacing the Roman provinces, Cicero wrote to the senate of his concern that the allied cities were wavering in expectation of a change in the established order in the region; there was little hope of raising troops through a local levy because they were either feeble or 'so estranged from us that it seems as though we ought neither to expect anything of them nor to entrust anything to their keeping' (*Letters to his Friends*, 15.1). When the Parthian attack failed to materialise, he embarked on military action against a hostile tribe called the Amanienses, burning their fortified posts, and besieged the town of Pindenissum, a stronghold of the Free Cilicians 'which has been at war as long as people remember'; the troops sacked the town, while Cicero received 120,000 sesterces from selling the prisoners (*Letters to Atticus*, 5.20.5). He took hostages from a neighbouring, equally hostile tribe, and arranged for his army to be billeted for the winter on newly-captured and recalcitrant villages (*Letters to his Friends*, 15.4.10). For all of Cicero's self-congratulation, there was clearly little expectation that the pacification of Cilicia would be concluded in the near future.

There were clear structural reasons why the Roman Republic could be open about the existence of sustained resistance to its rule; while one governor might declare that a province had been subdued as a result of his victories, his successor would have no compunction in contradicting that claim in order to obtain the troops and resources needed to deal with a continuing insurgency. Of course, the precise nature of this new emergency might be questioned; the main concern of most governors of a province like Spain or Cilicia was to seek out an opportunity for military glory on their own account, and a triumph might be awarded for actions that were little more than a raid on a hostile tribe. The two centuries which it took to subdue the Iberian peninsula, tying up 20,000–25,000 troops on a permanent basis, can be attributed as much to the incompetence, heavy-handedness and provocative behaviour of

Roman commanders, and the absence of any coherent plan for pacification, as to the qualities or temperament of the natives.[16]

Roman treatment of opposition was violent and destructive, with massacres, mass enslavement and the destruction of settlements – regardless of their beauty or historical significance, as in the sack of Corinth in 146 BCE or of Athens in 86 BCE (although in the latter case, the Roman commander, Sulla, prohibited the burning of the city). Rome's subjects had a clear idea of the consequences of rebellion and, nevertheless, some resented Roman rule sufficiently to ally themselves with powers like Macedonia or Mithridates of Pontus. In the west, the deterrent effect of the Roman treatment of defeated rebels was perhaps reduced by the fact that they could behave like that even when peace had been negotiated. On two different occasions in Spain, Roman commanders promised to resettle a tribe on fertile land and then took the opportunity when they gathered together to massacre a significant number and sell the rest into slavery.[17] On the first occasion, in 150 BCE, this triggered a widespread revolt that lasted over ten years until the Romans bribed some native envoys, sent to discuss peace terms, to assassinate their leader; on the second, it passed almost without comment.

Provinces were beaten into submission over decades, through the relentless and at times unpredictable application of military force, the gradual establishment of an infrastructure of camps and roads (built not for any peaceful purpose, but to facilitate troop movements in case of trouble) and the fear of subject communities that anything other than complete submission and cooperation might incur violent retribution. That is not to say that all Roman governors were treacherous war-mongerers looking for any opportunity to launch a punitive campaign, but a sufficiently large number of them were – and the Roman system encouraged rather than controlled this tendency – for it to be a permanent anxiety in all but the most peaceful of provinces. Even in Sicily, where the only military action after the Second Punic War had been the suppression of two large-scale slave revolts and where the governor relied on local levies rather than Roman troops, the threat of violent punitive action, examples of which continued to arrive from more distant parts of the empire, remained one of the crucial underpinnings of Roman domination.

The advent of the Principate and the establishment of autocratic rule under Augustus and his successors, following the civil wars of the first century BCE, brought Peace to the Empire. That was, at any rate, the declaration of the regime; its achievement was celebrated in the images on coinage, in literature and in programmatic monuments like the Augustan Altar of Peace (*Ara Pacis*) and the Temple of Peace constructed by Vespasian.[18] It became a recurrent theme in descriptions of the Empire and praise of the emperor. According to the historian Velleius Paterculus, 'the *pax Augusta*, which has spread to the regions of the east and of the west and to the bounds of the north and of the south, preserves every corner of the world safe from the fear of brigandage' (2.126.3); the encyclopaedist Pliny the Elder uses the phrase *immensa Romanae pacis maiestate*, 'the immense majesty of the Roman peace', as a synonym for the Empire (*Natural History*, 27.1.1), while the Greek orator Aelius Aristides waxed lyrical about the achievements of Rome in the middle of the second century CE:

> Wars, even if they once occurred, no longer seem real; on the contrary, stories about them are interpreted more as myths by the many who hear them. If anywhere an actual clash occurs along the border, as is only natural in the immensity of a great empire, because of the madness of the Getae or the misfortune of the Libyans or the wickedness of those around the Red Sea, who are unable to enjoy the blessings they have, then simply like myths, they themselves quickly pass and the stories about them. So great is your peace, though war was traditional among you.
>
> (*Oration 26 'To Rome'*, 70–1)

It should not be assumed that what the emperors and their propagandists were celebrating was identical with modern conceptions of peace. *Pax* in this context stood above all for the absence of civil war and the establishment of *concordia* at the heart of the Empire; it legitimised the replacement of the Republic with the rule of a single man, as the geographer Strabo argued early in Tiberius' reign:

> It is indeed difficult to administer a vast empire unless it is turned over to one man, as to a father. In any event, the Romans and their allies have never lived and prospered in such peace and plenitude as Augustus afforded them, from the time that he assumed absolute authority; and now his son and successor Tiberius continues his legacy.
>
> (*Geography*, 6.4.2)

Clearly the Empire was assumed to benefit from the absence of dissension amongst its conquerors and of freedom from the depredations of squabbling warlords, but the *pax* celebrated by the emperors as their gift to the world had a more direct relevance to the provinces: it stood also for successful conquest, the establishment of absolute Roman dominance.[19] Augustus' claim was that he had pacified, once and for all, the provinces of Spain, Gaul and Germany, as well as recovering provinces lost in the east and adding Egypt to the Empire (*Res Gestae*, 26–7). Vespasian's Temple of Peace commemorated the crushing of the Jewish revolt, the sacking of Jerusalem and the destruction of the Temple. Peace and empire were inextricably entwined, with imperial rule justified on the grounds that it brought peace – whether Rome's subjects wished for it or not – and peace defined as the absence of resistance. As Virgil's nationalistic epic put it: 'You, Roman, remember by your empire to rule the world's people (for these will be your arts), to impose the practice of peace, to be sparing to the subjected and to beat down the defiant' (*Aeneid*, 6.851–3).

It is easy to show that the positive image of the *pax Romana*, taken at face value by generations of modern historians, is at best optimistic; as the historian Tacitus put it, as part of his incisive critique of the monarchic regime, his history was 'violent with peace' (*Histories*, 1.2). It is abundantly clear from legal texts and other sources that neither banditry nor piracy were ever stamped out in the Empire; Roman control never extended effectively into mountainous regions, forests or deserts, from where unassimilated tribes and refugees from the Empire could launch raids into settled areas.[20] Civil war was scarcely eradicated, as seen after the death of Nero with the Year of the Four Emperors in 69 CE. Moreover, there are sufficient hints and passing comments in the sources to identify 100 or more examples of uprisings or revolts in the first two centuries of the Principate, from food riots in the city of Rome to full-blown rebellions in Gaul, to say nothing of famous revolts like Boudicca's uprising in Britain and the series of Jewish wars.[21] The gap between official rhetoric in the capital and the reality on the ground was clear enough to a disaffected observer like Tacitus. However, it would be misleading to dismiss the former as mere falsehood. Most ideologies exhibit a problematic relationship to reality, without that necessarily reducing their effectiveness. This one effectively characterised all opposition to the imperial regime as disturbers of the peace and the enemies of civil society, denying all legitimacy to their motives; it may well have worked to legitimise Roman rule in those regions which were largely spared serious disruption; and in particular it shaped the behaviour of the Romans themselves.

The Republican system had been readily able to accept that the process of pacification needed a further dose of military intervention, with minimal discredit even to the previous general; a revolt against the benevolent rule of the emperors, however, was deeply embarrassing to the individual who claimed full credit for establishing world peace. Augustus declined to make any report to the Senate about the campaign he had to fight in Spain in 26–25 BCE, and in his account of his own achievements presented the war against Sextus Pompeius in Sicily as merely an action against pirates. Tiberius, faced with a serious revolt in Gaul (which, according to Tacitus, left hardly any community untouched), chose to ignore it officially until the fighting was concluded, and then claimed that 'it would be undignified for emperors, whenever there was a commotion in one or two states, to quit the capital, the centre of all government' (Tacitus, *Annals*, 3.47). Thirty years later, in making a plea for Gallic nobles to be admitted to the senate, Claudius could claim that 'if you examine the whole of our wars, none was finished in a shorter time than that against the Gauls; from then on there has been continuous and loyal peace' (*Annals*, 11.24). The emperors and their subordinates displayed a similar tendency to self-deception or excessive optimism in the conquest of new territory, declaring mission accomplished after one successful campaign and apparently being genuinely surprised by any subsequent trouble. The massacre of Varus' legions in the Teutoberger Forest in 9 CE was a response to his attempts at collecting tribute and dispensing orders in the region of Germania; that is, treating it as a normal and fully pacified province and expecting its inhabitants to submit to his demands.

The natives were adapting themselves to orderly Roman ways and were becoming accustomed to holding markets and were meeting in peaceful assemblies. They had not, however, forgotten their ancestral habits, their native customs, their old life of independence or the power derived from weapons. Hence, so long as they were learning these customs gradually and by the way, one might say, under careful surveillance, they were not disturbed by the change in their way of life and were becoming different without knowing it. But when Quintilius Varus became governor in Germany and thus administered the affairs of those peoples, he strove to change them more rapidly.

(Dio, 65.18.2–3)

Resistance to Roman rule was generally presented as brigandage; that label stripped it of any legitimacy as a movement of protest, but it also offered the local commander a valid excuse for requesting reinforcements and resources, whereas admitting to the existence of a serious revolt would invariably be taken as a personal failure of the governor, since the alternative was to question the legitimacy of the entire imperial regime.

This fond belief in a rapid and irreversible progress from conquered territory to loyal province makes it difficult to discuss resistance to Roman rule under the Principate in any detail, since the sources scarcely discuss the subject. It is clear enough that the claims of Roman and Greek writers about the peacefulness of the empire cannot be taken at face value, let alone the belief of many modern historians that this absence of opposition or resistance can be attributed to the benevolence of Roman rule. However, the advent of the autocracy did lead to some significant changes in the Empire, besides an inability to admit to the possibility that anyone could conceivably resent Roman dominance. The rate of expansion slowed significantly. Augustus had advised his successor that the Empire should be kept within its existing boundaries (whether through fear or jealousy, as Tacitus suggested (*Annals*, 1.11), or for strategic reasons), and, while some emperors continued to pursue a policy of conquest, others preferred to consolidate territory or even, as in the case of Hadrian, to withdraw from a predecessor's conquests.

> Controlling the fairest parts of land and sea, they have on the whole tried to preserve their empire by diplomatic means rather than to extend their power without limit over poor and profitless barbarian tribes, some of whom I have seen negotiating at Rome in order to offer themselves as subjects. But the emperor would not receive them because they are useless to him.
>
> (Appian, *Roman History*, preface vii)

The process that had begun in the later centuries of the republic, whereby military glory ceased to be an essential source of political power and legitimacy, continued; expansionism ceased to be taken for granted as a goal, and became a matter of policy debate.[22] More importantly, the fierce competition for glory had largely ceased. Emperors had no contemporary rivals for status; they matched themselves against their predecessors or against an image of the ideal emperor, and so could be content with a single conquest in the course of their reign rather than year-on-year competitive slaughter.

At the same time, it was essential for them to prevent the emergence of potential rivals, by strictly limiting the opportunities of others for glory: triumphs were reserved for members of the imperial family (victories won by others were assumed to be achieved in the name of the emperor), while generals out in the frontier regions were strongly discouraged from taking any significant action without authorisation, let alone embarking on substantial campaigns. Expansion thus became more methodical and controlled, even – up to a point – more rational; the frontiers tended to stabilise in marginal regions, between settled agricultural areas that could easily support the Roman military infrastructure and wilder, emptier areas of forest or desert that promised to be expensive and unrewarding to conquer.[23]

Increased stability in frontier regions was echoed elsewhere in the Empire. Augustus' division of the provinces between those to be governed by senators, which involved no significant military activity, and those which remained under his direct control echoed the distribution of Roman forces and cemented tendencies already visible under the republic. Many regions – long-established and 'civilised' provinces like Achaea, Asia and Sicily, and the parts of Spain and Gaul longest in Roman hands – were assumed to be adequately pacified and far enough away from any significant enemy to risk leaving them without a substantial military presence. There is no evidence to support the idea that provinces were routinely and permanently disarmed; on the contrary, in the absence of a large body of Roman troops the governor would depend on recruiting soldiers locally to deal with any problems.[24] In other words, Roman peace was enough of a reality that large areas of empire could be governed effectively without regular recourse to direct force, with not only the acquiescence but the active collaboration of at least some provincials in enforcing Roman dominance.

COLLABORATION AND URBANISATION

Indeed, Roman government would have been entirely impossible without such local assistance. As late as the second century CE, the Empire was run by just 150 elite administrators, one for every 400,000 provincials. In comparison, British India in the nineteenth century was governed by around 7,000 administrators, one for every 43,000 natives, while under the Song dynasty in China, in the twelfth century, there was one official for every 15,000 inhabitants.[25] Of course, the Roman officials were supported by slaves and other assistants, but at the most these may have numbered 10,000, giving one representative of Roman power for every 6,000 of its subjects. The aims of Roman rule were strictly limited, focused on maintaining order and ensuring the continued flow of revenue, but even so it was impossible for such a small number of officials to manage all the day-to-day business of the control and exploitation of the provincials. Consideration of the geographical extent of the Empire and the effects of distance, in a preindustrial society where communications were limited to the speed of the fastest horse or most favourable winds and where the news of an emperor's death might not reach more distant regions for weeks, leads to the same conclusion: Roman rule depended on the delegation of power to the local level, not only to Roman officials, who had broad freedom of action in most affairs, but to their native collaborators.[26]

Thus the expansion of the Empire in the central and eastern Mediterranean depended on the establishment of friendly relations with hundreds of cities, each one dominating its immediate locality; preferably before conquest, but if necessary following a suitable interval after their capitulation, these could be granted autonomy in return for submission to Roman hegemony, contributions to Roman resources and assistance in the business of government. Rome entered into countless treaties with different states, kingdoms and city-states, generally on its own terms, whether or not they were formally incorporated into a province at that stage.[27] Centuries later, provinces like Sicily and Asia still displayed their origins in this piecemeal process of aggrandisement, appearing as patchworks of different sorts of allies and subjects with different statuses and privileges: free cities, cities with both freedom and exemption from taxes, allies and federates, Roman colonies, Latin colonies.[28] Most of these differences, with the exception of those cities who gained valuable exemptions from certain taxes or duties, related to status rather than to anything more material; all cities, even those officially 'free', were ultimately subject to Rome and therefore to the local governor – if he chose to intervene in their affairs. For the most part, however, governors respected local autonomy; cities were left to manage their internal affairs – finance, buildings, festivals, law and order – just as they had done before the arrival of Rome, so long as they managed them competently and did nothing that might jeopardise Roman interests. The Romans were happy to tolerate diversity in local organisation; in Greece, for example, they permitted cities to continue to hold popular assemblies to ratify laws passed by the local senate, although this was quite different from their own oligarchic model of city governance.[29]

The principles of Roman rule in such regions are clearly visible in the letters exchanged between the governor of Bithynia in Asia Minor and the emperor Trajan; the governor, Pliny the Younger, clearly possessed the right to intervene in local affairs and to impose his wishes on one or all of the cities in his province, but constantly sought reassurance from the emperor as to whether or not this was appropriate in any particular case. For example, he asked for a judgement on whether he should establish a uniform practice in the province regarding the payment of a fee by someone wishing to enter the local senate, 'for it is only fitting that a ruling which is to be permanent should come from you, whose deeds and words should live for ever'. Trajan replied:

> It is impossible for me to lay down a general rule whether everyone who is elected to his local senate in every town of Bithynia should pay a fee on entrance or not. I think then that the safest course, as always, is to keep to the law of each city, though as regards fees from senators appointed by invitation, I imagine they will see that they are not left behind the rest.
>
> (Pliny, *Letters*, 10.112–13)

In considering the relationship between Rome and the provincial cities, it is important to keep in mind that the Romans did not deal directly with the vast majority of their subjects. They sought to establish relationships with the dominant local elite, usually a status-conscious, city-based aristocracy whose power was based on birth, wealth, land ownership and the monopoly of religious and political offices – in other words, their own kind of people – and to rely on them to operate the local systems of control and domination. There were clear advantages for this elite, both individually and collectively, in cooperation with the ruling power, especially as it became clear that the loss of full autonomy was unavoidable in the face of Roman military power. They retained their position at the head of local society, and gained access to a wider range of material, social and even coercive resources with which to entrench their power. Frequently the interventions of Roman governors and emperors in the provinces were intended to bolster their supporters and reinforce their ties to Rome.

Individuals and their families were rewarded through grants of Roman citizenship, exemptions from taxes or duties, and other privileges, whether honorific titles or the right to collect certain dues from their fellow-countrymen; less formally, they might be favoured by the governor in court cases against their local rivals. Friendly cities might be granted special honours (given the status of a Roman colony, for example) or given grants to assist in public building projects, enhancing their status against neighbouring cities. Both of these processes can be charted in the epigraphic record, with inscriptions recording and advertising the achievement of civic status, the benevolence of the governor, the Roman affiliations of an individual family and so forth. In addition, the Romans might intervene to support the aristocracy as a collective, bolstering its coercive powers through the imposition of law and the occasional deployment of force to control crime or unrest; see for example Pliny's letter enquiring whether the town of Juliopolis might be given a small garrison of Roman soldiers, as had been done for Byzantium: 'Being such a small city it feels its burdens heavy, and finds its wrongs the harder to bear as it is unable to prevent them. Any relief you grant to Juliopolis will benefit the whole province, for it is a frontier town of Bithynia with a great deal of traffic passing through it' (*Letters*, 10.77). In this case the request was turned down on the grounds that all the cities in the province would want such a garrison; the governor was simply urged to be active in preventing injustice – that is to say, in maintaining the status quo and supporting the local elite.

The great advantage for the Romans in their implementation of this policy, in contrast to the experience of modern imperial powers, was the ease with which they could accept provincial aristocrats as allies and partners rather than merely subjects, and even allow them access to higher levels of power in the Empire. From an early date, Rome's conception of citizenship was quite different from that found in other Mediterranean city states, where the citizen body was a tightly-knit, homogeneous and exclusive group. According to one of its founding myths, the city's original growth was based on Romulus' creation of the Asylum, welcoming as full members of the community runaway slaves, exiles, criminals and anyone else who wished to join.[30] Either in homage to this principle, or as a policy that was then justified through the myth, in the course of their expansion the Romans granted citizenship (in several different forms, with varying rights to political participation) to individuals and allied communities in Italy and beyond; following the revolt of the allies in the early first century BCE (the Social War), they extended full citizenship to the whole of sub-alpine Italy. The rest of empire's population were not made citizens en masse until the third century CE, but over the previous centuries increasing numbers of provincials had already achieved this status, whether through individual grants or, in some cities, simply by serving as local magistrates.[31]

> There is that which certainly deserves as much attention and admiration as all the rest together. I mean your magnificent citizenship with its grand conception, because there is nothing like it in the records of all mankind. Dividing into two groups all those in your empire – and with this word I have indicated the whole civilised world – you have everywhere appointed to your citizenship, or even to kinship with you, the better part of the world's talent, courage and leadership... In your empire, all paths are open to all. It was not because you stood off and refused to give a share in it to any of the others that you made your citizenship an object of wonder. On the contrary, you sought its expansion as a worthy aim, and you have caused the word Roman to be the label, not of membership in a city, but of some common nationality, and this not just one among all, but one balancing all the rest... Many in every city are fellow-citizens of yours no less than of their own kinsmen, though some of them have not yet seen this city [Rome]. There is no need of garrisons to hold their citadels, but the men of greatest standing and influence in every city guard their own fatherlands for you.
>
> (Aelius Aristides, *Oration 26 'To Rome'*, 59–64)

The Roman attitude was almost entirely pragmatic; rather than applying any test of racial purity or ideological compatibility to potential collaborators, they looked simply for a comparable way of life and similar attitudes to their own, and rewarded extensive services and loyalty. Modern defenders of the British Empire, embarrassed by the contrast, remarked sourly that 'the Romans were not called upon to deal with large numbers of coloured races' and that 'it would be perhaps more accurate to say that all Roman citizens became lowered to the level of Roman subjects, than that all Roman subjects were raised to the level of Roman citizens', while cheerleaders for the United States pointed to its relative generosity in extending citizenship to aliens.[32] Meanwhile, the 'ideology' of provincial elites was simply their right to rule; there was no nationalistic, religious or ideological basis for sustained opposition to Roman hegemony, and none developed thereafter.[33]

Social divisions within the Empire were based primarily on wealth and status, not race or origin; able and ambitious provincials not only retained their local power but could aspire to the higher levels of the imperial hierarchy. Competition for local office became in some cases less an end in itself than a springboard for getting a family member into the Senate or the imperial service; some Greek sources made disparaging remarks about those who were not content with honour and glory in their own city but wished to be Roman senators (e.g. Plutarch, *Moralia*, 470C). The rewards for cooperation and conformity were an important factor, if not the most important factor, in the process of the adoption of elements of a common culture across the whole Empire, discussed in chapter 4. For the Romans, it meant that all those who might have spearheaded resistance to their rule were instead bound to them, individually and collectively, through ties of dependence and mutual advantage, and focused on competing with one another for prestige and advantage according to rules established by the Empire.

Roman rule, even in the most cooperative provinces, always combined sticks with carrots. The total number of Roman troops in the Empire was relatively small, as seen in the fact that they had to move legions between different frontiers according to immediate need, but their importance lay as much in creating the aura of power and the sense of threat as in any direct action.[34] Especially under the Republic and the early emperors, Rome sometimes intervened to reshape the provincial landscape for its own purposes, establishing colonies of settlers or former soldiers on confiscated land or amalgamating small cities into larger, more easily controllable centres.[35] This offered a means of punishing less favoured cities, while the threat of such action, on the whim of the ruling power, emphasised to provincials the importance of energetic collaboration:

> For some reason Augustus, perhaps because he thought that Patrae was a good harbour, took the men from other towns and collected them here, uniting with them the Achaeans from Rhypes, which he destroyed. He gave freedom to the people of Patrae and to no other Achaeans; and he also granted all the other rights and privileges that the Romans customarily give to their colonists.
>
> (Pausanias, *Description of Greece*, 7.18.7)

Much more important in the pacified areas of the Empire were the informal means of coercion; above all, intervention in the competitions within and between cities for prestige and imperial favour. Just as the governor or emperor might dispense honours, so they could withhold them, award them to a rival, choose one city rather than another to billet troops or requisition supplies, ignore or reject some petitions rather than others. The consequences of this policy of divide and rule can be seen in the flurry of letters and embassies from different cities on the accession of every new emperor, reporting on the erection of statues and the voting of new honours to him, seeking to have rights and privileges confirmed and to curry favour with the new regime, trying to strike the right level of obsequiousness. On the accession of Claudius in 41 CE, the city of Alexandria had particular need to grovel, following serious rioting between its Greek and Jewish populations, and Claudius' official reply shows the combination of condescension and veiled threat with which subject cities were kept in line:

Wherefore I gladly accepted the honours given to me by you, though I am not partial to such things. And first I permit you to keep my birthday as an Augustan day in the manner you yourselves proposed, and I agree to the erection by you in their several places of the statues of myself and my family; for I see that you were zealous to establish on every side memorials of your reverence for my household... As for the erection of the statues in four-horse chariots which you wish to set up to me at the entrance to the country, I consent to let one be placed at the town called Taposiris in Libya, another at Pharus in Alexandria, and a third at Pelusium in Egypt. But I deprecate the appointment of a high priest for me and the building of temples, for I do not wish to be offensive to my contemporaries, and my opinion is that temples and the like have by all ages been granted as special honours to the gods alone.

Concerning the requests which you have been eager to obtain from me, I decide as follows... It is my will that all the other privileges shall be confirmed which were granted to you by the emperors before me, and by the kings and by the prefects, as the deified Augustus also confirmed them... As for which party was responsible for the riot and feud...I was unwilling to make a strict enquiry, though guarding within me a store of immutable indignation against any who renewed the conflict; and I tell you once and for all that, unless you put a stop to this ruinous and obstinate enmity against each other, I shall be driven to show what a benevolent emperor can be when turned to righteous indignation.[36]

The Roman template for control was most effective in regions like Sicily, Greece and Asia Minor which had long been dominated by more or less autonomous city states and a clearly differentiated aristocracy, who could be recruited as collaborators. Elsewhere, the model had to be implemented more gradually. In Egypt, which had no tradition of self-governing cities, the Romans simply took over the system of bureaucracy established by the previous regime, recognising it as efficient and convenient for their purposes; urban centres were not granted any degree of independence or responsibility until the early third century CE.[37] Other regions, above all in the west, offered neither city-states nor any alternative form of administrative infrastructure; as they had previously done in parts of Italy, the Romans therefore sought to encourage changes in native society in order to make it more amenable to their rule.[38] Even before conquest, their influence was significant; studies of the peripheries of more modern empires has shown how tribalisation, generally assumed to be the traditional form of social organisation, is in fact a response to the proximity of an imperial power, as a previously diverse society with little in the way of social hierarchy gives power to leaders for the purposes of negotiation and war.[39] Having annexed the territory, the Romans looked to these tribal leaders to control the rest of the populace – effectively, through gifts of land, titles and other support, turning them into the kind of hereditary aristocrats, competing with one another for honour and status, with which they were familiar elsewhere. Cooperation provided these new elites with the prestige goods and other resources they needed to entrench their power – as indeed they had already been doing before the conquest, as revealed by the presence of unmistakably Roman items amongst the grave goods of some burials.[40]

This process was closely related to the progress of urbanisation; to judge from the archaeological evidence, the emergence and development of cities was a mixture of deliberate creation, Roman encouragement and spontaneous development. In Britain and northern Gaul, for example, roughly half of known *civitas* sites were founded on or near earlier native settlements, with others on the sites of military camps.[41] The establishment of an urban culture in the western provinces is often regarded as one of prime benefits of Roman imperialism for its subjects, and thus as a straightforward marker for the progress of civilisation in less developed regions.

Certainly Greek and Roman sources held the view that civilisation
was intimately connected to urbanism – note for example Strabo's
comments about the Gauls in the region of Massilia who 'became
more and more pacified as time went by, and instead of engaging in
war have turned themselves to civic life and farming' (*Geography*,
4.1.5).[42] One of the motives for the efforts of Roman governors to
promote city-building and to provide models for city organisation,
like the charters known from Spain, may indeed have been the wish
to lead provincial nobles towards proper conformity with Roman
values by encouraging them to adopt the correct constitutional and
social structures, in the expectation that this would influence their
behaviour.[43] But the tendency in Western culture to associate cities
with modernity and progress, and hence to regard urbanisation
as a good thing in itself, should not lead us to ignore its role in
establishing new orders of power in provincial society, and thus
entrenching Roman rule.[44] Tacitus offered a far more cynical view
of the process in England:

> In order that a population scattered and uncivilised, and propor-
> tionately ready for war, might be habituated by comfort to peace
> and quiet, he would exhort individuals and assist communities to
> erect temples, market places and houses; he praised the energetic,
> rebuked the indolent, and the rivalry for his complements took
> the place of coercion.
>
> (*Agricola*, 21.1)

Discussions of urbanisation, in both ancient and more modern
history, have tended to focus on attempts at defining 'the city',
whether according to ancient conceptions of the city as a political,
religious and social centre or modern ideas of the city as market
and industrial centre.[45] This can lead to fruitless arguments about
whether a particular centre meets the threshold criteria to be counted
as a 'proper' city, as well as reinforcing the Western myth that cities
are agents of modernisation, acting dynamically on any society in
which they are planted.[46] Rather, urbanisation is best understood
as an ongoing process, one of the products of the confluence of
four different processes of social, economic and cultural change:
concentration, crystallisation, integration and differentiation.[47] Each
of these processes of change is closely related to social power –
which is precisely why both the Roman state and various native
elites chose to invest a significant proportion of social surplus in
their development. The concentration of both people and resources

in nucleated settlements rather than scattered across the countryside made them easier for the local elite to control; the emergence of an urban hierarchy, as certain sites developed further because of their position within networks of exchange and information and smaller sites became increasingly dependent on them, gave power to those further up the hierarchy, above all to the city of Rome at its apex.[48] The 'crystallisation' of institutions (a better term than 'centralisation', since it is not necessarily a deliberate process), so that political, social, religious, cultural and economic institutions came to be co-located in the city, led to the overlapping and mutual reinforcement of different sources of power, all for the most part controlled by the same urban elite. Different forms of integration – drawing ever larger numbers of people into the same political institutions, eroding differences of language, customs and material culture, fostering the development of a social identity beyond that of kinship, drawing ever larger numbers of people into exchange networks and the market – created homogeneity out of diversity, and thus made the society more susceptible to rule. Economic differentiation made the concentration of people in cities possible, increased their interdependence and reinforced the power of those who controlled the bulk of the land and other resources; political and social differentiation reinforced the distinction between the elite and the rest of the population, and marked the former out as suited by nature and upbringing to rule the latter.[49] In summary, while the development of cities in the western provinces may indeed have had some beneficial economic and cultural consequences for the mass of the population (see Chapters 3 and 4), the Romans' primary motive in promoting urbanisation was self-interest: by encouraging their western subjects to become more like those in the central and eastern Mediterranean, they reinforced the power of the local elite over their people in order to make their own dominance as secure and cost-effective as possible.

Whether in the east or west, Roman rule had a significant impact on provincial society. Even where the Romans simply adopted and maintained local systems of dominance, they altered the conditions under which the local elite competed for power, and reinforced their control of the masses through access to power and resources, as well as new forms of coercion and ideology like the cults of Rome and of the emperors (see below, Chapter 4). At the same time, they risked undermining the relationship between elite and mass, whether through their demands for taxes or requisitions (which the elite had to extract from their people) or through the centripetal forces of Roman culture and power, so that an outward-focusing elite, adopting the trappings of 'Romanness', might become ever more alienated from the rest of the population. In other parts of the Empire, they sought to introduce a whole new structure of society and new forms of social and political behaviour, conforming to their own expectations, with a dramatic increase in the power of the elite over the rest; in order for their potential collaborators to be useful, they had to be given the power to coerce and exploit their people on the Romans' behalf.

Inevitably this provoked resistance, especially when the changes were rapid and far-reaching, as is suggested by the accounts of revolts in Germania and Gaul. The crucial question is how long such resistance may have lasted, once it ceased to take a violent – and hence historically visible – form, especially as the literary sources and inscriptions from the provinces were generated by those who had thrown their lot in with Rome. As noted above, while Rome always held the threat of military action in reserve, there is little trace of political or military opposition in the pacified regions; historians have sought instead to identify resistance to 'Romanisation' in the patterns of consumption amongst the wider population that are revealed by the material evidence. For example, the decline of the urban centres known as the *civitas* capitals in Britain from the second century CE has been interpreted as resistance to the rule of the pro-Roman tribal elite.[50] The great advantage for the Empire in its chosen style of domination was indeed that, for the most part, any hostility would be directed against the local elite who had to implement their demands and collect their taxes or who took advantage of their privileged position to oppress and exploit the population. Once the initial disruption of conquest was past, the Romans ceased to be the clear enemy; it seems entirely possible that their domination was effectively invisible to the majority of the population, a matter of regular concern only to the client ruling class.

In general, serious problems arose only when the Romans encountered unfamiliar forms of society; as they did elsewhere, they fixed upon the group that looked most like their kind of aristocrats, to the exclusion of any other influential groups, and sought to promote them as proxy rulers regardless of their actual level of popular support. In first-century CE Judaea, the most important example of this, they favoured the Jewish landowning aristocracy and largely ignored those who held religious authority – the idea that these two sources of power could be entirely separate was alien to Greco-Roman culture. The aristocracy struggled to impose its authority on the populace, and was thus increasingly ignored by the governor; seeking an alternative source of power, Jewish nobles courted popularity by leading resistance against Rome instead.[51] The Jewish revolt had a number of different causes, above all the conduct of Roman officials and a lack of respect for religious sensibilities (not least Caligula's wish to have a statue of himself installed in the Temple), but the crucial difference from other provinces was that the Romans sought to rule through people who should never have been entrusted with power. In Gaul and Britain, meanwhile, the Romans first ignored the Druids, favouring a more traditional warrior aristocracy as their collaborators, and then sought to exterminate them as a source of power and influence separate from the aristocracy and not integrated into Roman rule. They were more successful here than in Judea, but the question remains whether pacification might have been more or less straightforward if they had been willing to show flexibility in their approach to provincial rule.

ROMAN PROVINCIAL GOVERNMENT

Roman administrative structures were minimal, keeping the costs of empire low, because most tasks were outsourced to local collaborators, and because the aims of Roman rule were equally minimal: to maintain order or at least prevent outright conflict, to maintain the flow of taxes and recruits, and to ensure continuing submission. The Romans felt little sense of any obligation to their subjects. Taxes and tribute were collected as the reward for their dominance and as recompense for the expenses of conquest. At best, they offered the logic of protectionism, levying taxes in return for the absence of war, as Cicero wrote to his brother:

> The province of Asia must be mindful of the fact that if it were not a part of our empire it would have suffered every sort of misfortune that foreign wars and domestic unrest can bring. And since it is quite impossible to maintain the empire without taxation, let Asia not grudge its part of the revenues in return for permanent peace and tranquillity.
>
> (*Letters to his Brother Quintus*, 1.1.34)

The belief of later historians, especially in nineteenth-century Britain, that Roman imperialism was driven by a mission to bring civilisation to the unenlightened barbarians was entirely misplaced. The Romans certainly noted the impact of their rule on provinces in the west, but in so far as they encouraged aspects of this development it was entirely for their own ends, and left largely in the hands of the provincials. Even in the city of Rome, which benefited from the spoils of empire in the form of public buildings and a reliable grain supply, the ancient state took upon itself few of the activities or responsibilities associated with modern states – education, housing, economic management, poor relief, health – and thus it had no need for any elaborate infrastructure. In the provinces, the minimal obligations of the ruling power to the masses (provision of public sacrifices and festivals, action in case of major food crisis) were left almost entirely to local notables.[52]

Indeed, by modern standards Roman provincial government was almost entirely unsystematic and amateurish. Roman governors received no formal training in administration or financial affairs, having been appointed as the result of political machinations in the senate or of the emperor's favour, and their staff was made up of dependents and friends rather than professional administrators.[53] That this was possible, with remarkably few adverse consequences in the course of the Empire's history, was due to the nature of their task: not administration but negotiation and politicking, balancing the competing demands and interests of different cities, different factions within those cities and other groups in provincial society, including tax farmers and Roman and Italian ex-pats, whether settlers or merchants. Cicero's summary of his achievements in Cilicia gives a clear indication of the expectations of the governor's task: 'I have rescued the communities and have more than satisfied the tax-farmers. I have offended nobody by insulting behaviour. I have offended a very few by just, stern decisions, but never so much that they have the audacity to complain' (*Letters to Atticus*, 6.3.3). The essential skills for the job were those of a skilled politician, not an efficient administrator, and the Roman political system was an ideal source of such men.

The governor had broad freedom of action within his own province, and was not even bound by precedents set by his predecessor. This was a Roman tradition, deriving from the old idea of the magistrate's *imperium*, the expectation of obedience, but it was also a necessity to enable him to respond effectively to unpredictable situations, especially given the length of time it might take to inform Rome of a problem and receive further instructions. The same can be said of his role as the highest judge and arbitrator within the province, aiming to balance the interests of justice (as he saw it) with more pragmatic considerations about the identities of those involved and the likely reaction of different groups to a particular decision. Much of this power was held in reserve; most governors, especially under the Principate, preferred to avoid action despite the entreaties of different cities or petitioners, precisely because it might upset the balance between competing elements, and their role in the law was tempered by the expectations of the provincials and the complex relationship – the creative tension, as it has been suggested – between Roman and indigenous law and custom.[54] The governor's power was limited too by the size of the province relative to his resources; his inability to be everywhere at once, and hence his reliance on local aristocrats for information – which must almost invariably have been distorted or censored in their own interests. Furthermore, he was always caught between local and central demands, and – at least to judge from the correspondence between Pliny and Trajan – chronically short of resources:

> Pliny to Trajan: Will you consider, sir, whether you think it necessary to send out a land surveyor? Substantial sums of money could, I believe, be recovered from contractors of public works if we had dependable surveys made...
> Trajan to Pliny: As for land surveyors, I have scarcely enough for the public works in progress in Rome or in the neighbourhood, but there are reliable surveyors to be found in every province, and no doubt you will not lack assistance if you take the trouble to look for it.
>
> (*Letters*, 10.17, 10.18)

Under the Principate the governor faced both ways, representing the emperor to the provincials but also representing his province to the centre, aware of how its behaviour might reflect on his own stewardship and hence affect his standing with the emperor:

> Pliny to Trajan: We have celebrated with appropriate rejoicing, sir, the day of your accession, whereby you preserved the Empire; and have offered prayers to the gods to keep you in health and prosperity on behalf of the human race, whose security and happiness depends on your safety. We have also administered the oath of allegiance to the troops in the usual form, and found the provincials eager to take it too as a proof of their loyalty.

Trajan to Pliny: I was glad to hear from your letter, my dear Pliny, of the rejoicing and devotion with which under your guidance the troops and provincials celebrated the anniversary of my accession.
(*Letters*, 10.52, 10.53)

The Roman approach to provincial government was flexible, easily accommodated to local circumstances and, above all, cheap, but there were some obvious flaws in the system – not only for provincials, but even for Rome. Firstly, the process of appointment of governors did not necessarily yield the most skilled politicians for each province; some assignments were fought over fiercely, and won by those candidates best able to marshal support and call in favours, but less popular and lucrative regions were given to anyone who couldn't evade the fact that it was their turn (Cicero, for example, was deeply reluctant to shoulder the burden of governing Cilicia, despite his self-presentation as one of most noble and self-sacrificing of Roman notables). Under the Principate, meanwhile, imperial provinces might be assigned according to the whims of the emperor's patronage, and success in toadying to a single absolute ruler to win an appointment was not necessarily replicated in dealing with the competing demands of provincials. Secondly, governors' terms of office were generally short, barely a year under the republic: there was thus no continuity in the administration (since the governor's staff were attached to him rather than the province), little opportunity to develop administrative ability or knowledge of the province and its people, and no need to shoulder the burden of mistakes – Cicero openly expressed his wish to avoid a prolongation of his duties in Cilicia, on the grounds that he had gained as much glory as was available and risked losing it as a result of unexpected events. The situation improved gradually under the Principate, with longer terms of office becoming the norm, but now a governor could be recalled at a moment's notice as a result of imperial whim or any change in the balance of influence in the imperial court.

Most notoriously, the wide powers of the governor and the nature of his task created enormous opportunities for abuse in the cause of personal, rather than state, enrichment. This is implicit even in accounts of exemplary governors, like Cicero's self-presentation or Tacitus' account of his father-in-law Agricola:

He decided therefore to eliminate the causes of war. He began with himself and his own people: he put in order his own house, a task not less difficult for most governors than the government of a province. He transacted no public business through freedmen or slaves; he admitted no officer or private to his staff from personal liking, or private recommendation, or entreaty; he gave his confidence only to the best. He made it his business to know everything; if not always to follow up his knowledge; he turned an indulgent ear to small offences, yet was strict to offences that were serious; he was satisfied generally with penitence rather than punishment; to all offices and positions he preferred to advance the men not likely to offend rather than to condemn them after offences.

(*Agricola,* 19.1–4)

This encomium reveals some of the typical deficiencies of other governors, even those who were basically honest and well-intentioned; it is misleading only insofar as it implies that the problems were entirely due to a lack of moral fibre or common sense, rather than to the nature of the system. Above all, the governor might well be ignorant (wilfully or not) of what was being done in his name, as his subordinates took advantage of the power gained from their proximity to power, their access to the governor and their ability to filter the information he received. As was also the case at the heart of the Empire, the volume of business was greater than any individual could manage; those who managed the governor's paperwork had significant influence on which cases were given priority. The evidence suggests that most corruption in the legal system was not aimed at affecting the outcome of cases but at moving them up the queue for consideration.[55]

The governor's subordinates were generally appointed through personal or family connection. In theory, that placed them under personal obligation to him, but it might equally tie his hands in dealing with their misdemeanours; a nephew, or the son of a powerful ally, cannot be dealt with in the same way as an incompetent or corrupt bureaucrat. Roman society was organised around complex networks of friendship, influence and patronage, operating through favours, obligations and unwritten expectations of reciprocity and gratitude: according to the philosopher Seneca, the exchange of services and favours – *beneficia* – was the basis of social cohesion.[56] This affected not only the governor's relations with his staff but also much of his day-to-day activity. To judge from their correspondence, both Cicero and Pliny spent much of their time as governors dealing with letters, requests and introductions from friends and other connections, all of which implied or assumed that they should make use of their power on the writer's behalf. Cicero, for example, received a letter in Cilicia from a friend, demanding that he should arrange for large numbers of panthers to be sent to Rome for the games, and then continuing:

> I recommend to you M. Feridius, a Roman *eques*, the son of a friend of mine, a worthy and hard-working young man, who has come to Cilicia on business. I ask you to treat him as one of your friends. He wants you to grant him the favour of freeing from tax certain lands which pay rent to the cities – a thing which you may easily and honourably do and which will put some grateful and sound men under an obligation to you.
>
> (*Letters to his Friends*, 8.9.4)

It was hardly in the interests of the Cilician cities to lose a portion of their revenue; Cicero declined to grant this request, but plenty of other governors might have done so, as a means of reinforcing a friendship, building up obligations and maintaining their client base. Under the republic, it is clear that governors faced a particular issue in managing their relations with the *publicani*, the contractors who had bought up contracts for provincial tax collection and who inevitably sought to make largest possible profit on their investment, at the expense of the provincials. Cicero was explicit about the dilemma:

> If we oppose them, we shall alienate from ourselves and from the state an order that has deserved extremely well of us... and yet if we yield to them in everything, we shall be acquiescing in the utter ruin of those whose security, and indeed whose interests, we are bound to protect.
>
> (*Letters to his Brother Quintus*, 1.1.32)

> Apparently you want to know how I handle the tax-contractors. I cosset them, I defer to them, I praise them eloquently and treat them with respect – and I see to it that they don't bother anyone... So the Greeks pay at a fair rate of interest and the *publicani* are very pleased because they have full measure of fair words and frequent invitations from me. So they are all my intimate friends and each one thinks himself especially favoured.
>
> (*Letters to Atticus*, 6.1.16)

Furthermore, the governor had to judge his relationships with different provincials, deciding which ones to trust and favour in order to keep the province manageable. In his long list of advice to his brother on provincial government, Cicero advised caution in dealing with those who profess deep friendship and affection for the governor, 'especially when those same persons show affection for hardly anyone who is not in office, but are always at one in their affection for magistrates' (*Letters to Quintus*, 1.1.15).

In your province there are a great many who are deceitful and unstable, and trained by a long course of servitude to show an excess of sycophancy. What I say is that they should all of them be treated as gentlemen, but that only the best of them should be attached to you by ties of hospitality and friendship; unrestricted intimacies with them are not so much to be trusted, for they dare not oppose our wishes, and they are jealous not only of our countrymen but even of their own.

(*Letters to Quintus*, 1.1.16)

It is easy to imagine the temptation for the governor, obliged by his duties to establish relationships with both the leading families of his province and the *publicani*, to show favouritism to his friends, fall into compromising situations or find himself under obligation to particular individuals or cities. It is equally easy to imagine the opportunities for personal enrichment that a less scrupulous governor could find in his position, above all in the need for provincials to seek his favour and avoid his displeasure. Cicero's famous prosecution of Gaius Verres for misconduct in his term as governor of Sicily offers numerous examples, and makes it clear that most of the time there was no need for the governor even to threaten legal action, let alone to abuse his powers, in order to exact compliance – a simple request, with the authority of the governor behind it, was generally sufficient. Verres is said to have tried to seduce the daughter of a provincial notable by billeting one of his underlings in the household (*Against Verres*, II.1.65–9); to have seized works of art from private individuals by asking to borrow them so that he could inspect them, or simply ordered communities to hand over statues on public display (II.2.88); and to have fraudulently claimed the estates of wealthy men after their death (II.2.35–49). He accepted bribes to alter a verdict (and then condemned the man anyway, in Cicero's view an even worse crime than simple corruption; II.2.78), bribes to allocate a seat in the local senate and a post as a priest (II.2.123–4, 127), bribes to alter the tax assessment of rich individuals and to exempt particular cities from supplying sailors or ships – but he did then have a merchant ship built for himself at the expense of the city, to carry off his ill-gotten gains (II.2.138, II.4.21, II.5.20, II.5.61). An entire section of one of Cicero's speeches (II.3.162–228) dealt with Verres' abuses in the collection of corn for Rome: money sent from Rome to buy corn was embezzled; Sicilian farmers were forced to hand over whatever level of tax the collectors demanded (they could go to law to apply for a reassessment afterwards, but that was scarcely a realistic possibility for most); rather than requisitioning corn for the upkeep of his own household as was expected, Verres demanded money instead and levied this at a rate far in excess of the market price for corn. The cities were intimidated into silence; the *publicani*, who had benefited from their share in the excessive exactions, passed a resolution to expunge any of their records that might be damaging to Verres' reputation.

It is worth noting that Verres did make some attempt to cover his tracks; this level of abuse went beyond the limits of acceptability even in Rome, not least because some of his actions were directly contrary to Roman interests, and there was at least a theoretical possibility that a corrupt or abusive governor could be held responsible for his actions. Under the republic, he was immune from prosecution during his term of office; in theory, an appeal could be sent to the senate, which might set up an enquiry or send out an embassy, but in practice they would respond only to most powerful, above all the groups of *publicani*, not to mere provincials. After his term of office a governor could be prosecuted, as Verres was, back in Rome, but it is clear from the speeches that a successful prosecution was very rare. Cicero listed the range of expedients, including the appointment of a tame prosecutor and attempts at delaying the trial for as long as possible by starting a rival prosection, which were available to someone who had amassed sufficient funds and allies during his time in office. The corrupt governor's greatest protection, however, was the tendency of senators to support their own, and to regard a certain level of extortion, provided that it was not too obvious, as part of the privileges of office. Cicero noted the widespread perception 'that these courts, constituted as they now are, will never convict any man, however guilty, if only he has money' (I.1).

A conviction – or, in the case of Verres, a fear of conviction leading him to flee into exile – depended less on the strength of the prosecution's case or the level of abuse than on external circumstances. The main hope for provincials was if the accused had powerful political enemies who would seize upon an excuse to attack him; Cicero's case, meanwhile, succeeded because the senate was threatened with losing control of the extortion court and so needed to be seen to put its own house in order. Under the Principate, provincials had the right of appeal to the emperor, but that was unlikely to be effective against one of his favourites and could have repercussions; their condition was effectively subject to the emperor's whims and to court politics. In either period, they might be better advised to keep quiet and accept a certain level of extortion – or, since the provincial cities themselves were rarely united, to seek to win the governor's favour and so direct his greed towards their rivals. Cicero's remark on this subject was intended to shame his fellow senators into, for once, convicting one of their own, but it reflects a basic truth about the nature of Roman provincial government:

> I said I believed the day would come when our foreign subjects would be sending deputations to our people, asking for the repeal of the extortion court. Were there no such court, they imagine that any one governor would merely carry off what was enough for himself and his family; whereas with the courts as they now are, each governor carries off what will be enough to satisfy himself, his advocates and supporters, and his judges and their president; and this is a wholly unlimited amount. They feel that they may meet the demands of a greedy man's cupidity, but cannot meet those of a guilty man's acquittal.
>
> (I.41)

THE EMPIRE'S LONGEVITY

Corruption is not necessarily a problem for a society if it is moderate and predictable; as noted above, Roman society constantly trod the fine line between gifts and bribery, friendship and favouritism, reciprocity and corruption. The need for flexibility and judgement, rather than strict regulation, was even enshrined in law:

> A proconsul need not entirely refrain from 'guest-gifts' (*xenia*), but only set some limit, not to refrain entirely in surly fashion nor to exceed the limit in grasping fashion... For it is too uncivil to

accept from nobody, but contemptible to take from every quarter, and grasping to accept everything.

(*Digest*, 1.16.6.3)

Extortion and corruption became a serious problem for provincial government only when they upset the balance between different groups, creating disorder and disrupting tax collection; in other words, when the private interests of the governor came into direct conflict with the interests of Rome. Under the Principate, the nature of oversight shifted from the regulation of friends and colleagues by former and aspiring governors in the senate to the regulation of his subordinates by the emperor. There was an increase in the number of officials with specific financial responsibilities, above all for managing the vast imperial properties and for collecting taxes; these were equestrians and occasionally freedmen, not senators, and so directly dependent on the emperor and (in theory) less likely to pursue their own interests to any great extent.[57] Part of the motivation for these changes may have been to improve the quality of government and to protect the provincials from exploitation – the emperors did, after all, present themselves as the protectors of the whole Empire, and draw legitimacy from this – but at least as important was the need to maximise imperial revenue and to prevent any governor or general from gaining too much power and so becoming a threat. Nevertheless, the problems of distance and the slowness of communication meant that the emperor was always reliant on the reports of his own officials, only occasionally supplemented by other reports or petitions from the province. The Empire was too large, the technology too limited and the administrative structure far too sparse to permit intensive regulation or control.

Rather, Roman rule worked on the basis of a confluence of interests: it was in the interests of local elites to cooperate and to keep their populations quiet, it was in the interests of governors to keep their provinces well-behaved and so to moderate their rapaciousness, and it was in the interests of the Empire as a whole to limit its interference in local affairs. Each party gained a share of whatever surplus could be extracted from the mass of the population. The local rulers perhaps had to settle for a smaller share than they had enjoyed during periods of full independence, but instead they gained access to Roman power and resources and the opportunity to aspire to higher office as part of the imperial system. The Empire and its rulers had to settle for a smaller share than they might have been able to extract, but were spared the costs of administration that would have been involved in establishing direct control rather than working through intermediaries.

Cooperation was underwritten by fear, based on Rome's reputation for violent retribution against rebels and its known capacity for applying overwhelming force – which was of course much cheaper than actual military intervention. It was supported by the lack of unity of the Empire's subjects – Rome dealt, through its governors, with a host of individual communities, separated from one another politically and culturally and encouraged through the selective distribution of favours to compete with one another – and the way in which Rome and its culture became the sole unifying factor. Roman rule was above all pragmatic, enriching its rulers through the creation of a trans-Mediterranean kleptocracy in which local agents were recruited to fleece their own peoples in return for the opportunity to become Roman and join those higher up the social pyramid. The development of this system of cooperative parasitism took place over a long period; there was no dramatic change under Augustus, but rather the techniques of collaboration and mutual advantage that had been used in Italy and the eastern Mediterranean for centuries were applied to the western provinces once their social structures had been sufficiently transformed under Roman influence. The passage of time cemented the arrangement, as local elites became ever more integrated into Roman structures and their cooperation became a matter of habit, tradition and a shared culture and symbolic order, rather than a pragmatic decision taken to secure their own position in local society.

The Empire lasted so long because, early in its history, as Rome first began to expand its influence in Italy, it developed a model of rule that was flexible enough to work in almost all situations. As long as the costs of administration and military activity were kept low, the benefits of collaboration remained sufficiently high, and the mass of the population produced sufficient surplus to keep all the different groups of their exploiters content and cooperative, there was no obvious reason why the Empire should not be indefinitely sustainable. Roman peace – even if, for the vast majority of the population, this was the peace enjoyed by the domesticated animal, kept solely for what it could produce – was an enduring reality.

3
'The Emporium of the World': The Economic Impact of Empire

Whatever is grown and made among each people cannot fail to be here at all times and in abundance. And here the merchant vessels come carrying these many products from all regions in every season and even at every equinox, so that the city appears as a kind of common emporium of the world. Cargoes from India and, if you will, even from Arabia the Blessed one can see in such numbers as to surmise that in those lands the trees will have been stripped bare, and that the inhabitants of these lands, if they need anything, must come here and beg for a share of their own.

(Aelius Aristides, *Oration 26 'To Rome'*, 11–12)

Many modern theories focus on the relationship between imperialism and economic structures and processes. Economic factors are often seen as one of the motors of modern imperialism; this may be seen in terms of 'trade before the flag' and the influence of commercial interests on persuading the imperial power to pursue a policy of annexation, or of the encounter between societies at very different levels of economic and technological development causing social upheaval and creating a situation that draws the imperial power into intervention, or of the dynamics of capitalism leading to a crisis of over-accumulation and a search for new outlets for production.[1] Other studies focus on the consequences of imperialism for economic development in colonised regions. One tradition emphasises the positive effects of the transformation of traditional (for which read 'primitive') forms of agriculture and craft production, as the result of the transfer of more advanced technology and techniques, the influx of capital, the construction of infrastructure like railways, bridges and roads and the integration of the colonised region into a wider economy.[2] Imperialism is seen to operate, deliberately or accidentally, as an agent of modernisation, providing the resources and political will to overcome impediments (whether material, institutional or cultural) to full economic development. In due course it may become an impediment itself, restricting the liberty of the colonial subjects and isolating the colonised region from the full range of market opportunities by locking it into an exclusive relationship with the imperial power; but, at least in the early stages of the process, imperialism is claimed to play an essential role in overcoming inertia and resistance to economic transformation.

More critical and sceptical perspectives generally offer two different lines of argument. The first is to question positive evaluations of the impact of the imperial power on the economy of its possessions: both the extent of disruption caused by the initial annexation, with the widespread destruction of property, people and indigenous economic structures, the seizing of land and the displacement of large numbers of families; and the continuing restriction of economic development and individual initiative, partly as a means of control and partly, it is argued, in the interests of the manufacturers and merchants of the imperial power.[3] The second is to question the idea that 'development' – invariably understood as development according to the Western model – is intrinsically desirable, because it imposes a particular set of technology, techniques and institutions that may be ill-suited to local conditions, and leaves farmers vulnerable to food crises because they are encouraged or compelled to grow cash crops for the market rather than ensuring their own subsistence.[4] Theories of 'underdevelopment' and 'dependency' draw these two strands together: the consequence of imperial control, it is argued, is that the colonised region is locked into a subordinate position within the world economy, prevented from modernising fully so that it continues to supply raw materials to the industrialised nations rather than competing with them in the production of higher-value goods.[5]

One key issue for these debates is the difficulty in distinguishing between the effects of capitalism (or, more generally, modernisation) and those of imperialism in shaping the historical development of non-Western countries. For writers who see the two as separate, albeit often closely connected, influences on colonised regions in the nineteenth and early twentieth centuries, there is a significant analytical problem in determining how far local developments may be attributed directly to imperial rule rather than to the effects of integration into the developing world economy. The process of modernisation has affected regions that were never under direct Western control, such as China, in ways that are often similar to developments in regions like India or Africa; and of course it has continued long after the formal withdrawal of imperial powers from their possessions. This is less of a problem for Marxist accounts, which regard modern imperialism precisely as a process within capitalism and are happy to talk of 'neo-imperialism' in the post-colonial world; for example, when discussing the role of global institutions such as the World Bank and International Monetary Fund, whose policies are heavily influenced by the United States, in imposing a particular model of economic development on countries and in ensuring optimum conditions for the operations of (foreign) capital there.[6]

Rome has played little role in such debates about the relationship between empire and economy, except as a point of contrast with modern developments. In the late eighteenth century, Adam Smith had argued that the relationship between Rome and its colonies should serve as a model for Britain's policy towards the Americas because it was positive and productive for both parties.[7] He and other early political economists noted the development of trade and craft production in various areas of the ancient Mediterranean, but regarded such changes as occurring despite, rather than because of, Roman imperialism. The wealth of Rome, James Steuart argued, like the wealth of Babylon and Persia, was the product of conquest and thus proved to be the ruin of those states, whereas cities like Athens, Carthage and Alexandria had enjoyed genuine industrial and commercial development.[8] Rome was dominated by slavery and despotism, with the commercial and industrial classes subordinated to the military and landowning elite, and their anti-economic ethos: 'the policy of the ancient republics of Greece, and that of Rome, though it honoured agriculture more than manufactures or foreign trade, yet seems to have rather discouraged the latter employments than to have given any direct or intentional encouragement to the former'.[9] Rome's wealth was therefore consumed unproductively, and the provinces were bled dry of resources and population to fuel the luxurious lifestyles of its rulers, rather than encouraged through the development of exchange to improve their systems of production. Imperialism was not intrinsically opposed to economic development in the view of these writers, but an imperialism of conquest and domination, under the command of a despot, would do nothing to promote an increase in prosperity in either the provinces or the imperial heartland.

The classical political economists did not see the Roman economy as qualitatively different from that of their own society; thus the limited development of trade and manufacturing in the Empire could serve as a useful lesson to contemporary society about the necessity of political liberty and a rational approach to national prosperity. Within a generation, a radical shift in attitude had occurred, as economists and historians became convinced of the uniqueness of modern economic development, and perceived a yawning gulf between the present and all previous societies.[10] Commentators eulogised modern productive power and identified a range of different characteristics of the modern economy – the application of science and technology, the development of institutions such as banking and credit, the organisation of labour, economic rationality and knowledge of the workings of the economy – that were absent, or scarcely developed, in earlier times. The Roman economy was clearly pre-industrial, primitive and limited, ignorant of the maxims of political economy and dominated by non-productive motives; it therefore ceased to be of any interest to contemporary discussions, including those focused on imperialism. Ancient historians meanwhile embarked on a lengthy debate about how far the ancient world could be considered proto-modern and how far it should be seen as utterly different.[11] If they related their studies to the present, it was generally to consider the 'failure' of antiquity to develop along modern lines, focusing on the absence of those elements identified as important for the emergence of capitalism in the early modern period. In so far as the role of Roman imperialism was considered, it was seen in negative terms, either for the failure of the Roman state to pursue rational economic policies or, more commonly, for its deadening effect on individual freedom and entrepreneurship and the development of the free market. The Empire was regarded as parasitic, creaming off the wealth of the provinces in booty and taxes and offering little or nothing in return.[12]

Although understanding of the Roman economy has been distorted by constant contrasts with modernity, so that it is more often presented in negative terms as 'not-modern' rather than being described in its own terms, the contrast between the two societies is real and significant: Rome remained a pre-industrial and pre-modern society, vastly inferior in material terms.[13] It depended on the produce of the land not only for food but for most raw materials and for most of its sources of power – wood, and the food to support human and animal muscle; in the absence of advanced technology and chemical fertilisers, there were strict limits on the extent to which the productivity of either the land or labour could be increased.[14] The vast majority of the population therefore worked on the land and lived close to subsistence level, producing a low level of surplus beyond the needs of their family and so able to support only a small level of demand for manufactured goods; the high-pressure demographic regime, with a high birth rate offset by a high death rate (especially infant mortality), meant that any increase in production would normally be counteracted by an increase in population rather than a rise in real incomes and living standards. The Mediterranean environment was capricious, characterised by alternating glut and dearth, and transport and communications were slow, expensive and unreliable; the market functioned erratically at best, so that – for entirely rational reasons, rather than being a sign of a primitive mentality – economic motivation focused on risk avoidance and the satisfaction of needs rather than maximising profit.[15]

However, this pessimistic picture can be exaggerated: the fact that classical antiquity entirely lacked the exponential economic growth that has characterised the modern era does not mean that growth was unknown.[16] The 'limits of the possible' in a pre-industrial economy were undoubtedly restrictive, but within those limits there was wide scope for variation in the performance of different societies, there is evidence to suggest that Rome may have performed at a higher level than many contemporary and later societies.[17] If the Roman economy did develop significantly, then it is worth considering how far and in what ways this may be connected to the establishment of the Empire. This line of thought has been encouraged by two relatively recent developments in contemporary economic theory. Firstly, there has been an upsurge of interest in the economic consequences of integration and connectivity, with globalisation seen as the essential basis for development. The Roman Empire was drawn together, however loosely, into a single political space; it seems entirely possible that this may also have become a single economic and cultural space, which would have had significant implications for the workings of economic structures and the lives of its inhabitants. Secondly, there has been a focus on the role of institutions, especially the state, in creating the conditions necessary for economic growth, in opposition to theoretical approaches that regard the state as a significant impediment to the beneficial operation of the free market.[18] The Roman state was certainly one of the most important economic actors in ancient Mediterranean, given its command of resources and the geographical extent of its influence, and so its actions must have had an impact on economic development in general – whether positive or negative. The Empire had sufficient power to overcome the 'limits of the possible' in at least some circumstances and to take actions that could ease them in the longer term for at least some of its inhabitants; it could reshape the conditions under which individual economic actors made their decisions. It was equally well placed to restrict certain developments if they appeared to threaten its own position, and for its actions to produce unintended consequences.

This was never a directed process; the Romans had no conception of 'the economy' as an analytical category, little understanding of its operations beyond a hazy grasp of such simple phenomena as the relation between supply and price, and no notion that it was part of the task of government to promote prosperity or encourage industry. Insofar as the Roman state made decisions that could be termed economic, such as managing taxation, they were taken solely in its own interest: protecting its income and the interests of its ruling class, managing state resources, ensuring that the army and the capital were properly supplied and that the army was paid. However, as far as development was concerned, the motivation for these decisions was far less important than their effects. This is the major implication of Aristides' description of the city of Rome, quoted above. Rome grew because it was the capital of the Empire, magnifying imperial power, and the centre of the activities of the political elite; it was a centre of consumption, not of production. The flows of taxes and rent on which it subsisted made it a rich and attractive market, especially as the grain supply was subsidised so that sectors of the population enjoyed a higher level of disposable income. As a consequence, it drew in supplies from the whole world, making some people very rich – the description of the fall of Babylon in the book of Revelation, generally agreed to be a fantasy of the fall of Rome, offers a similar perspective to Aristides' account:

And the merchants of the earth weep and mourn over her, for no man buyeth their merchandise any more... The merchants of these things, who were made rich by her, shall stand afar off for fear of her torment, weeping and mourning, saying: 'Woe, woe, the great city... for in one hour so great riches is made desolate.' And every shipmaster, and every one that saileth any whither, and mariners, and as many as gain their living by sea, stood afar off, and cried out as they looked at the smoke of her burning, saying, 'What city is like the great city?' And they cast dust on their heads, and cried, weeping and mourning, saying, 'Woe, woe, the great city, wherein were made rich all that had their ships in the sea by reason of her costliness'.

(Revelation, 18.11–19)

In this, as in other ways, the rise of Rome had a dramatic impact on the economy of its empire. The crucial question is whether its impact was essentially parasitic, stripping the provinces and even regions beyond the Empire of their resources through its command of wealth and power, or whether its influence was sometimes more positive; whether Roman globalisation was a force for economic development, or simply a more powerful means of exploitation.

THE REWARDS OF CONQUEST

The most unmistakable consequence of Roman imperialism was the transfer of resources from the conquered provinces to the centre on an astonishing scale. Conquest, especially of the wealthy kingdoms of the east, brought booty: the defeat of Macedonia in 167 BCE collected 120 million sesterces' worth (the equivalent of 120 senatorial fortunes), while the treasury of Mithridates, captured by Pompey, contained 860 million sesterces. Especially in the west, conquest also led to the transfer of hundreds of thousands of people as slaves. Regions that were incorporated into the Empire had to pay taxes and tribute in money and goods; other regions, such as the cities of Greece and Asia in 70 BCE, were forced to pay indemnities; resources taken under state control, such as the silver mines of Spain, brought in millions every year. By the time of Augustus, Rome ruled – and appropriated a share of the produce of – 60 million people or more, its revenues having risen by at least a hundredfold in two and a half centuries. Roman taxes were relatively low, perhaps 5% of gross produce, partly because the state offered little in return and partly because it was necessary to leave a sufficiently large share of the peasants' surplus for the local elites; nevertheless, the Empire commanded enormous resources, which cemented its dominance.[19]

Not only the Roman state but also its leading members became extremely wealthy as a result. In Cicero's time, a reasonably well-to-do senator was said to need an annual income of several hundred sesterces; by Pliny the Younger's day, the average income was over 1 million sesterces, while by the fourth century some senators drew in 6–9 million sesterces every year.[20] Roman and Italian aristocrats acquired extensive estates overseas; by the time of Nero, six senators were reputed to own most of Africa – an exaggeration, but not too incredible – and the passing of successive laws to force senators to have at least some of their wealth invested in Italy shows how far the economic interests of Rome's elite had become globalised.[21] Elite families used this wealth as the basis for further accumulation, funding the political activities of their members to win more opportunities for gaining booty and glory, or simply acquiring ever larger estates and portfolios of urban properties, investing money in funding commercial ventures and so forth. The Roman elite's notorious disdain for merchants was directed against those who were directly involved in day-to-day business activities; they had no objection to making large amounts of money, even from commerce, by working through agents.[22]

The primary significance of this accumulation of wealth was that it led to far-reaching changes in the location and the nature of demand within the Empire: the ways that the Roman state and its aristocracy chose to spend the resources gathered from the provinces shaped the dynamics of the economy. As noted above, ancient peasants were unable, because of the limitations of technology and the nature of their environment, to produce more than a small surplus above what they and their families consumed. However, the aggregate surplus of 60 million people is a significant level of resource; what really matters is how and where it was consumed. Because of the uncertainties of the climate and the unreliability of market mechanisms, producers might prefer, if left to their own devices, to store their surplus rather than sell it to buy other goods; those items which they could not make themselves were generally produced locally, because of the costs of transport and because no region enjoyed a sufficiently large comparative advantage in their production. The result was that there was only limited scope for the development of large-scale inter-regional specialisation or trade, and little incentive either for the improvement of agriculture or the development of industry. Most farmers lacked the resources and, above all, sufficient land to make it worthwhile investing in improved technology or even buying an ox, because the animal would simply replace family labour which would still have to be fed, and because there was insufficient reliable demand for the produce to cover increased costs.

There was always some trade around the Mediterranean, because certain goods (metals, for example) were not found everywhere, and because the vagaries of the climate created periodic food crises and hence a market for grain.[23] However, this trade remained for the most part small-scale, based on small boats with mixed cargoes hopping from port to port along the coast and on itinerant pedlars with a wagon or a few pack animals. More specialised trade, or trade on a larger scale, was a high-risk occupation, subject to the vagaries of the weather and the market in an environment where information was hard to come by and expensive; and so market and industrial activity remained a thin veneer over a largely agrarian, subsistence economy.[24] Roman imperialism transformed this situation by gathering the surplus produce of different regions and concentrating it at particular locations, creating centres of demand for goods that could not be supplied solely from the immediate locality. Resources that might otherwise simply have been consumed by their producers now supported an expanding infrastructure of redistribution and market activity, and provided a livelihood for a substantial class of intermediaries.

The first centre of demand was the army: the largest and most important item in the imperial budget, constituting perhaps half or more of total annual expenditure, since keeping the 300,000–400,000 soldiers properly supplied was essential both for the security of the Empire (and hence for the legitimacy of the imperial regime) and for the security of individual emperors. The total number of soldiers was small relative to the total population of the Empire – and far inferior to the level of mobilisation achieved by modern European regimes – but because the majority were stationed in sparsely populated frontier regions, often at the margins of successful cereal cultivation, feeding them was a major logistical problem.[25] Some supplies could be obtained locally – and the proportion must have increased over time, as frontier regions developed their cereal production in response to the army's presence (this certainly happened in Britain, as is clear from the archaeological record) – but a substantial quantity of grain always had to be transported from the most productive regions (Sicily, Africa and Egypt above all) to the margins of the Empire.[26] Soldiers enjoyed a relatively high standard of living, with the basic diet of grain supplemented generously with pork, cheese, vegetables, olive oil, salt, spices and sour wine; the more perishable goods had to be found locally, the rest were imported – and, as the distribution of Spanish oil amphorae and wine amphorae from Italy, Gaul and Spain shows, transported over long distances. The army also required horses and pack animals, which needed fodder; leather for most of its equipment (it has been estimated that the army in northern Britain consumed 12,000 calves per year just to repair and replace its tents) and metal for the rest (excavation of a single legionary fort in Britain has produced 20 tons of iron nails, to say nothing of armour and weapons).[27] Whether these supplies were acquired through taxation in kind and requisition, or obtained through the market by contractors, this represents a substantial and regular transfer of resources from the richer inner provinces of the Empire to the frontier regions.

The second centre of demand was the city of Rome, which grew from around 200,000 people in the second century BCE – already an impressive size for a pre-industrial city – to nearly 1 million by the time of Augustus, a figure unsurpassed in Europe until the beginning of the nineteenth century.[28] Rome's growth was based entirely on its role as imperial capital, first as the arena for competition between the aristocracy (conducted through public and private building projects, lavish entertainments for the population and conspicuous consumption in their private lives) and then as the playground of the emperors, magnifying the glory of the Empire and their own prestige through building projects and largesse. It was never an industrial or commercial city in the sense that those activities were the basis for its existence, but it supported a large population of craftsmen, employed in the service of the elite and the state and above all in their construction projects, and a large number of traders and others involved in the task of feeding this population and providing different services. Rome required at least 150,000 tonnes of grain every year, 75 million litres of wine and 20–30 million litres of olive oil, to say nothing of meat, vegetables and other produce, and firewood, demands which could never be met from the city's immediate hinterland; it also drew in marble, bricks, timber, metal, animals and slaves from across the Empire, all funded by the taxes, rents and booty drawn from the provinces. Like the army, Rome benefited both from the redistribution of goods collected as tax in kind or produced from state lands, mines and quarries, and from the purchasing power of the state and the elite in the market.

Thirdly, there were the new cities discussed in the previous chapter, supporting the power of the emerging elites in the west. It is generally agreed that there was a substantial increase in urbanisation under the Empire, in terms both of the number of urban centres and their size (including the expansion of existing cities); it is impossible to offer more than a rough order of magnitude, but perhaps 12% of the Empire's population lived in centres of several thousand people or more by the early Principate.[29] Not all of these people worked in crafts or other non-agricultural occupations, but most of them must have done, and so had to be fed from the produce of others; furthermore, one effect of the concentration of population was that resources had to be spent on transporting food from its place of production and on creating the infrastructure for its mobilisation and distribution. Like Rome, these cities were arenas for elite competition and expenditure, which supported a population of craftsmen and builders and those who provided services for them. Some, especially the major ports, became prosperous because of their location at strategic points in the supply networks of the Empire, siphoning goods out of their region towards Rome or the army; others developed an important role in the manufacture of particular goods because of their location, on the sea coast in the case of the production of fish sauce, at the edge of pastoral regions in the case of textile production.[30] Above all, however, it was the Romans' cultural and political preference for city life that brought into being a concentration of population and resources in the urban centres, and hence the need for some form of redistribution.

Fourthly, there were changes in the patterns of consumption across the Empire: new demands for different sorts of goods which could not be satisfied locally. These changes are most visible in the case of the elite, especially in the western provinces, who invested heavily in new forms of conspicuous consumption like villa-style country residences and the consumption of wine; this was part of the process of differentiating themselves from the rest of society as the basis for their dominance and identifying themselves with the ruling class of the Empire.[31] However, the archaeological evidence for the widespread distribution of wine amphorae and fine-ware pottery from Italy suggests that other sectors of the population also changed some of their habits. The Gauls, for example, had acquired a taste for Italian wine even before the Roman conquest, but the expansion of the Empire spread this habit across the western Mediterranean – partly as a consequence of the diffusion of a new preference for bread rather than porridge, which meant that people needed to drink more.[32] The dynamics of these various cultural changes, and the extent to which they should be thought of as 'Romanisation', will be considered in the next chapter. Clearly, however, the economic implications of millions of peasants choosing to spend part of their surplus produce on manufactured and imported goods – a small amount individually, perhaps a single piece of fine pottery in a year and the occasional cup of wine, but a substantial level of demand in aggregate – were far-reaching.

THE DEVELOPMENT OF CONNECTIVITY

Both directly, through its military activities, and indirectly, through its development of the imperial capital and its impact on the provinces, Rome created centres of demand for goods that could not be satisfied from local production, either in terms of volume or, frequently, in the type of goods. This demand was satisfied in a number of different ways. In the case of the army, some of these supplies were gathered as tax in kind from grain-producing provinces, or requisitioned rather than purchased. That left little scope for the 'military multiplier' to boost economic activity through incentives to producers and merchants – except that the supplies then had to be transported from the place of production to the frontiers, and Rome possessed neither a merchant marine nor a state transport corps. The state had to hire the owners of ships or pack animals (or to requisition them in return for a fee) for the purpose.[33] Other army needs were met by hiring contractors to manage the whole business of sourcing, purchasing and transporting supplies. In the case of the city of Rome, the state took responsibility for part of its grain supply, distributing some of the grain it collected as tax from Sicily, Africa and Egypt to a privileged sector of the population (eligibility was based on citizenship, not on poverty); like the grain for the army, this had to be transported by privately-owned ships.[34] In other words, state redistribution always worked of necessity in cooperation with private enterprise, rather than in opposition to it. Indeed, the state effectively subsidised private commerce, offering incentives for the construction of more and larger ships to be used for carrying state supplies (which could also be used for private enterprise) and for signing up to supply contracts, in which the owners were paid at market rates and could transport private goods alongside their official cargoes and on the return voyage.[35]

Traders who assist in supplying provisions to the city, as well as shipowners who service the grain supply of the city, will obtain exemption from compulsory public service, so long as they are engaged in activity of this sort; for it has very properly been decided that the risks which they incur should be suitably recompensed or rather encouraged, so that those who perform such public duties outside their own country with risk and labour should be exempt from annoyances and expenses at home; as it may even be said, that they are absent on business for the state when they serve the grain supply of the city.

(*Digest of Roman Law*, 50.6.5.3)

The task of supplying the city of Rome with foodstuffs besides grain and with most raw materials was almost entirely in the hands of private enterprise; some wealthy landowners might transport produce from their country estates to their urban residence, as part of the Roman idealisation of rustic self-sufficiency, but the mass of the population depended on merchants and shopkeepers for their food.[36] The city was an enormous and lucrative market for almost any sort of product; the limited evidence for ancient prices suggests that those in Rome were significantly higher than elsewhere, at least in the western Mediterranean, as would be expected, reflecting both the wealth of the city and the costs of transport.[37] Above all, shipping goods to Rome was free from the usual uncertainties about demand and price; whereas trade in a single commodity usually entailed the possibility of finding on arrival in port that the market had collapsed and the cargo had to be sold at a loss (taking into account the costs of transport and of paying back any loan used to buy the cargo in the first place), Rome and other great cities offered a more or less guaranteed profit.

In Rome, as in other major cities (and many minor ones), the authorities took further measures to encourage merchants to supply their markets – measures that were entirely in their own interests, but which nevertheless served to promote trading activity. They constructed market buildings; stalls were presumably rented out, as a contribution to civic revenue, and the concentration of activity made it easier to regulate and tax, but this benefited traders by advertising their presence to consumers.[38] They invested in harbour facilities; a port which offered merchants shelter from storms was likely to be more regularly frequented, enhancing both local revenues and the city's access to resources. In Rome, where the logistical nightmare of moving large volumes of goods from merchant vessels moored outside the sandbar at the mouth of the Tiber into barges, and of the weight of traffic up and down the river, was one of the main risks to the city's food security; this entailed the construction of a series of enclosed harbours, wharves and warehouses on the coast, and the development of an entire town, as well as procedures to keep the river properly dredged and the lines of barges flowing smoothly.[39] Other infrastructure was developed by the state for purely military purposes, to facilitate the movement of troops, army supplies and information; but roads and canals (for example, the canal built by Marius to improve access at the mouth of the Rhône) were open to all, including traders, and made it cheaper and easier to transport goods.[40] Some of these new transport arteries worked to intensify existing traffic; others created connections between previously isolated areas, and so opened up new regions of the Empire to trade and Roman influence.[41] The unification of the Mediterranean reduced the risk of a trader's cargo being seized by a foreign power in the event of war. Finally, the importance of the state grain supply and the need to assert their dominance across the Mediterranean led the Romans to conduct military operations against pirates and bandits; the long-term efficacy of these actions is in doubt, as low-level criminal activity seems to have been endemic under the Empire, but if nothing else they may have reduced the fear of attack and so encouraged trade.[42]

The risks of piracy, shipwreck and unfavourable markets were not the only impediments to the development of trade; there was also the danger of being cheated. If the costs of measuring the value of the object of exchange, protecting the rights of all those involved and policing and enforcing agreements – what are termed 'transaction costs' – were too high, then it was preferable not to attempt a transaction in the first place. The development of any exchange beyond small-scale, highly personalised deals between members of the same community depended on the development of an alternative to simple trust as the basis for deals; the cheaper and more reliable that alternative was, the easier it was for exchange to develop.[43] Here again the state and the local city administrations played a vital role, in establishing institutions that reduced uncertainty and hence reduced transaction costs. In the interests of public order, for example, they established means of resolving disputes through the courts and enforcing the court's judgement, and sought to prevent disagreements developing in the first place through the development of the law. Over the centuries, Roman law developed ever more flexible and sophisticated procedures for sales, introducing the concept of 'good faith' and supporting such complex transactions as the sale of a share in the wine to be made from the grapes currently hanging on the vine. Roman contract law covered the complexities of terms for loans and undertakings for services; the law of agency covered the issues that might arise from the preference for managing business through agents, including slaves, and the degree of responsibility retained by the master for actions carried out in his name.[44] Roman law was often reactive rather than proactive, with new concepts and precepts being developed by the magistrates in response to cases that appeared before them; the steady development of the law related to commercial transactions is evidence of the expansion of commercial activities in the Empire as much as it was one of the contributing factors to that expansion. It should be stressed that the law was not developed in order to facilitate trade, and in some respects it could be an impediment: only individuals of citizen status could make contracts that were fully binding (which might explain one of the attractions of gaining citizenship), and the more complex the law became, the greater the costs involved in trying to make use of it, either in drawing up contracts or in trying to enforce them. Because court cases were decided by magistrates, it may be suspected that members of the elite might enjoy a certain advantage in legal disputes; furthermore, the laws limiting the liability of masters for the actions of their slaves would seem to benefit those who regularly worked through such agents rather than those who had to deal with them. For dealings between equals, however, Roman law was an invaluable tool; it offered standardised procedures for conventional transactions, and the existence of the possibility of legal action must have ensured that most agreements were kept more or less honestly by those involved.

The authorities also provided standard forms of measurement, reducing the costs involved in establishing the weight or volume of the goods to be exchanged; this may have originated in order to regulate the collection of taxes, but the system was clearly useful for other purposes, and inscriptions found in the market areas of many different cities record the donation of weights and measures by local notables. Most importantly, the state issued coinage; this was a means of paying soldiers and state officials, a convenient form in which to exact fines or taxes, a means of propaganda and an assertion of state power – but it had enormous economic implications.[45] Money offered a standard and easily divisible measure of value for transactions; coined money provided a convenient means of exchange, with the value of the coins established and guaranteed by the state (so, for as long as there was sufficient faith in the state, there was no need to pay for the metal content to be assessed; it was illegal to refuse to accept coins that bore the head of the emperor). Further, coins served as a convenient way of storing wealth, which might encourage a farmer to convert his surplus into a less perishable form by entering the market. The Romans had certainly not invented coinage, but they spread its use throughout the western Mediterranean (army service seems to have been one important driver of monetisation, as soldiers spent their pay in frontier areas and those from non-monetised regions sent part of their wages back home). Most importantly, the Roman state created a single monetary area across the Empire, with centrally-produced gold and silver coins supplemented by local minting of smaller denominations; the removal of costs associated with money-changing, both the direct charges (normally around 5%) and the uncertainties about exchange rates and value, represented a further reduction in overall transaction costs. The volume of coinage in circulation across the Empire increased dramatically to unprecedented levels; there is no evidence of any significant price rises before the third century at the earliest, so this must reflect some combination of increases in the volume and value of goods in circulation and increases in the velocity of circulation, both signs of the expansion of the monetised market economy.[46] The Roman economy is sometimes assumed to have been constrained by the absence of bills of exchange, bank notes and other negotiable instruments as a means of transferring capital between regions, but there is no evidence for such constraint; on the contrary, the absence of such financial instruments may be a sign that the state's issuing of coinage was more than adequate to support the Empire's economic activity – whether or not that was ever the conscious intention of the system.

The security of the Empire depended on connectivity, the (relatively) rapid and reliable movement of goods, people, information and money across a wide area; it thus used its resources to create conditions that then enhanced the connectivity of the Mediterranean for all its inhabitants. The result of these developments and of the creation of new centres of demand was a dramatic expansion in the volume of goods being moved around the Empire from the second century BCE onwards, charted through the increase in the number of identified shipwrecks from different periods and through the vast numbers of amphorae found hundreds of miles from their place of manufacture.[47] Some merchants must have become rich from their involvement in different forms of trade; at least one is known to have gained entry to his local city council, despite the uniform attitude of disdain for trade found in the literary sources.[48] Most traders recorded in the sources or found in inscriptions were of only middling status, substantially more prosperous than the typical peasant but far inferior to the landed elite – and of course there must have been many too poor to leave any trace in the record. It is possible that the process of distribution was too fragmented, with too many intermediaries taking a share of the profits; the greatest fortunes were made by those who not only financed the most lucrative voyages but also made money from production and from the leasing of commercial properties, the traditional elite. Ancient Rome did not see the emergence of merchant princes or giant multinational companies, but it did experience a high level of trading activity across the whole of the Empire.

TECHNOLOGY AND INNOVATION

The Roman Empire was characterised by an unprecedented scale and level of efficiency in the redistribution of resources, through a combination of direct state action and private incentives. The results were manifest in the extension of political and military power, the expansion of cities, the scale of public building and the lavish lifestyles of the elite. The key question is how far this represented no more than a concentration of the existing level of surplus production in the hands of the state and the political elite, with a share going to those who collected and transported this surplus on their behalf, and how far there may have been an increase in productivity and hence in the level of surplus – in other words, whether the cake grew larger so that the increased consumption of the ruling powers was not necessarily at the expense of the masses. Some of the goods being moved across the Empire were collected as taxes or rents in kind, usually as a proportion of the total harvest, which offered no incentive to producers to change their methods to increase productivity. However, many goods were mobilised through the market, with merchants buying up supplies in urban and rural markets or directly from the producer. Farmers and manufacturers were therefore made aware of the existence of an increased demand for their products and of the possible profits from increasing production; conventional development economics argues that, all other things being equal, they should have responded by seeking to increase production through additional inputs of labour and capital, especially the use of new technology.

Clearly, these new economic conditions did not bring about a Roman industrial revolution; the Roman Empire remained agrarian, dependent on organic sources of energy and thus severely restricted in its capacity for growth. However, a strong case can be made that the unprecedented transformation of the modern economy is what really requires explanation, rather seeing it as a natural development and hence regarding earlier societies as failures because they did not undergo the same radical changes. Furthermore, we need to consider all evidence for changes in different areas of production, rather than concentrating on those associated with later developments.[49] For example, there is no evidence of the mechanisation of harvesting grain in Mediterranean agriculture; there was no pressing need for it because it would be incompatible with the frequent practice of inter-cultivating crops, labour was for the most part not commoditised and the climate meant that generally the harvest could be carried out in a leisurely manner. However, one literary source refers to a reaping machine in Gaul, where the threat of storms made it practical to invest in devices to save time and labour; there is, unfortunately, no evidence as to how widely the machine was adopted.[50] There was, on the other hand, significant technical innovation and substantial investment in equipment for processing crops, with the development of the screw-based wine press, the oil press, and grain mills operated first by animal power and later by water wheels.[51] This includes some exceptionally large constructions, like the Barbegal grain milling complex in southern France and substantial oil processing installations in Africa.[52] The Romans were not hostile or indifferent to the possibilities of productive technology, but employed it where it would be useful and profitable; mechanisation was ill-suited to Mediterranean agriculture, but it could make a significant impact on the costs and efficiency of processing crops, and so repay the investment. Industrial production similarly remained unmechanised – with the exception of bread-making; to judge from the carvings on the tomb of a prosperous baker from Rome, some establishments made use of a form of kneading machine, which would represent a substantial saving in labour.[53] Most strikingly, there was extensive technical development in mining in Spain, with human-powered bucket wheels to remove water from the shafts (as far as 30 metres, in some cases), the construction of reservoirs above the workings from which water was released to wash away the spoil from the ore, and mechanised ore-crushing; Roman engineering expertise enabled the exploitation of much deeper seams than had previously been possible, and made the process much more efficient on a grand scale.[54]

For the most part, however, technical innovation was incremental, based largely on the extension and refinement of existing techniques. Production was intensified through the application of fertiliser: from animals, at least on those farms large enough to support them, from humans (the inhabitants of the farm and, in the neighbourhood of urban centres, external supplies) and from growing and ploughing in 'green manures', rather than simply allowing land to remain fallow. Techniques of grafting, transplanting and training tree crops, olives and vines were widely diffused, not least through the agricultural handbooks published by Roman authors, drawing on Greek and Carthaginian works and their own experience. New varieties of crops were developed, to maximise yield or suit particular conditions; comparison of the lists in manuals from the first century CE with those in earlier works shows that farmers had an increasing choice, and were urged to select varieties according to the local environment.[55] Iron tools were familiar enough, but archaeological evidence suggests that they became more widely diffused through Italy and the western provinces. Inscriptions and archaeological evidence from Italy and north Africa reveal the systems used to manage the key resource of water; not only the aqueducts that brought in urban supplies (and were, to judge from the complaints of one official in the capital, frequently targeted by farmers seeking to appropriate a share of the water) but channels, dykes and mechanisms for diverting water to different fields, and social and political institutions (including the law) for managing the conflicts that would inevitably arise in times of shortage.[56]

Even within the existing technical limits of Roman agriculture, there was scope for significant expansion of production. Archaeological survey evidence shows how previously marginal land was brought into cultivation; in some areas, that must simply reflect an increase in population – but in the vicinity of major cities like Rome, and in regions that are known to have exported products in substantial quantities, it must also reflect the influence of the market, either because producers were seeking to maximise production, or, equally plausibly, because the most fertile land was being taken over by cash crops for the market. This process is most visible in the *suburbium* of Rome, which was characterised by the intensive production of fruit, vegetables and other perishable luxuries for the urban market – in fierce competition with the demands of other users, especially the political elite who also profited from catering to the city's demands (the so-called *pastio villatica*, from capons and honey to dormice and game) but who were primarily interested in leisure and comfort.[57] Other urban centres saw a similar intensification of settlement, presumably in conjunction with intensification and specialisation of production, in their immediate hinterlands.[58] Other regions of Italy saw an increase in wine and olive oil cultivation in the later centuries of the Republic, and the agricultural manuals – although of course we have no idea how widely they were read or how often their advice was followed – placed increasing emphasis on production for the market and on the profits to be made from farming.[59]

Beyond the suburban market gardens, this did not amount to full specialisation; even the market-orientated villas of the agronomists were to produce the full range of different crops, aiming to supply most of the needs of their workforce without having to rely on external supplies, and the practice of growing a range of crops as a defence against harvest failure must have remained ubiquitous amongst the peasantry. However, there were changes in the choice of crops and the balance between them, most significantly a shift from barley to wheat as the main grain crop; barley was much less susceptible to drought, and hence a better choice for the self-sufficient peasant, but wheat made better bread, and so it is difficult not to see this change, and later the adoption of naked rather than hulled wheats, as a response to market demand.[60] In the western provinces, meanwhile, the Roman period was characterised by the diffusion of the set of crops associated with Italian agriculture, to the limits of their ecological niches: the expansion of grain cultivation in Britain and frontier provinces, driven by the demands of the army; the introduction of viticulture into Gaul and Spain, so that over time locally-produced wine replaced most Italian imports and was exported to Rome in substantial quantities; and the dramatic expansion of olive oil cultivation in Spain and Africa, again not only coming to replace imports but also taking a substantial share of the imperial market.[61] A similar pattern can be charted in industrial production in Gaul, as imported fine-ware pottery was progressively replaced by local imitations as they came to be of sufficiently high quality – and, arguably, as the level of demand increased.[62]

There were still strict limits to regional specialisation; it remained the case that most goods could be produced anywhere in the Empire, certainly within every region if not in every part of it. The major channels of movement of goods were therefore either to the main centres of demand, or to regions still in the process of developing their cultivation or production; true inter-regional trade, once the western provinces had caught up with the rest of the Empire, was found primarily in specialised items like fish sauce, incense or spices that could be produced in only a few places. At the same time, there is no evidence for underdevelopment in the modern sense, no restrictions placed on development or any compulsion on the provinces to produce only raw materials for the industrialised centre – because, obviously, the centre itself was barely industrialised. In the absence of any comparative advantages, Roman economic development tended to level out as each province developed its own means of producing the goods it had previously had to import.

FORMS OF EXPLOITATION

The most significant structural changes as a consequence of Roman imperialism were in the organisation and exploitation of labour.

In the course of the Roman conquests, and subsequent actions to pacify provinces and suppress revolts, millions of captives – men, women and children – were sold into slavery: reduced to the status of property, uprooted from their homes and transported to Italy and Sicily, where they were subjected to the complete dominance of their new owners and the constant threat or reality of violence, usually for the rest of their lives. The continuing demand for slaves also fuelled a substantial peace-time trade that continued long after the Empire had ceased to expand, drawing in fresh supplies from across the frontier and encouraging slave-owners to breed their own replacements.[63] There is no reliable basis for determining total numbers, but even the most minimal estimates, based not only on the figures quoted for war captives but on study of the demography of slavery and the level of replacement necessary to keep the numbers steady, suggest a figure in the region of 2–3 million, at least a quarter of the total population of Italy.[64] In the last two centuries of the Republic, Italy was transformed into a slave economy. That does not mean that slaves did all the work – most of those working the land were still free peasants, and the cities would not have expanded to the extent they did if the migrants had no prospect of employment – but rather that slavery was an essential part of the economic structure, above all because of its importance for the wealth accumulation of the land-owning elite. Even before this, Rome can be classed as a slave society, organised around structures of dominance and control, whose ideology was built around the distinction between freedom and slavery and highly sensitive to – if not thoroughly obsessed with – issues of power and status.[65]

Modern discussions of Roman slavery since the eighteenth century have tended to focus on their employment in agriculture, and above all in the villa, the intensive market-orientated estate worked by slaves under the supervision of a slave overseer. This area of activity has yielded the most detailed discussions of the operation of slavery, in the agronomists' handbooks (though slavery is taken entirely for granted by these authors, and the slave workers receive little more attention than any of the other animals on the estate; the main focus is on the problematic role of the *vilicus*, the slave entrusted with the supervision and control of other slaves).[66] Equally importantly, the emergence of this form of economic organisation in central Italy in the second century BCE is ascribed a major role by both ancient sources and modern historians in the crisis of the Roman peasantry and hence in the political conflicts of the late Republic; the alleged displacement of peasants to make way for slaves has been compared with the English enclosure movement as an overt example of class warfare.[67] Furthermore, the villa has offered a test case for seeking to understand the ancient institution of slavery; there have been long debates about whether the Romans employed slaves because they conferred status or because they had to do something with their war captives, because there were insufficient free workers (either because of the crisis of the Italian peasantry, this time attributed to the effects of Rome's constant military campaigns, or because free men regarded wage labour as slavish) or because slaves were more profitable or productive.[68]

Some of these arguments are easily answered: the Romans could have ransomed their prisoners, and sometimes did; the decision to sell them into slavery implies the existence of substantial demand, offering higher prices than the captives' families could offer. The countryside was not emptied of peasants, despite the claims of certain populist Roman politicians, as seen both from archaeological survey and from the fact that the villas relied on employing casual labour from the locality at harvest time, as a means of keeping the size of their permanent workforce to a minimum. The idea that wage labour was slavish and to be avoided at all costs comes from elite sources, and it is questionable how far it may have penetrated through the mass of the population; certainly this contempt for honest work was the dominant ideology in Rome, but equally clearly there were plenty of wage-earners in the cities, some of whom were proud enough of their activities to advertise it on their tombstones.[69] The importance of slave-owning as a source of status is undeniable, but that does not exclude the existence of economic motivations as well; it is the nature of a slave-owning culture that slavery influences and is determined by all areas of life. What is undeniable is that the Roman agricultural writers do not ever question the place of slaves at the heart of their enterprises; they do not even discuss alternative forms of labour, except for poor land in unhealthy areas or more distant estates, where tenants might be preferred – emphasising that slaves were an investment, to be employed where they would be most profitable, and not to be exposed to excessive risks of premature death.

There are clear indications that the villa mode of cultivation was intended to be highly profitable, and the nature of the labour force was a crucial part of this. Managing a medium-sized estate directly through slaves was certainly more profitable than letting the estate to a number of tenant farmers; all surplus production was profit for the owner, whereas the level of rent would be much lower because of the farmers' need to feed their families. The villa was large enough to permit some division of labour, aiding efficiency, and for some workers to develop specialised skills like vine-dressing; there was no risk of a slave worker moving elsewhere after his training in search of higher wages. Slaves could be compelled in a number of ways – force or the threat of force, the issuing and withholding of privileges – to work harder and longer, and to work under conditions of close supervision – even as part of a chain gang – that might have been intolerable to free men.[70] The limited evidence for prices suggests that slaves were generally expensive, except in the immediate aftermath of a military campaign, and it is clear that the intensive management of the villa was costly, with the master expected to visit regularly to monitor the performance of his overseer; for this to represent a practical investment, the returns must have been considerable, through the reduced costs of maintenance compared with wages, and perhaps through productivity gains as a result of employing 'thinking tools'.

The intensive slave villa was a limited phenomenon in geographical terms; the costs and risks were balanced by the profits to be made from supplying the city of Rome and the western provinces, but only for those with easy access to the sea, so that transport costs remained low. Archaeological survey reveals striking differences in the patterns of settlement between regions immediately along the Etruscan coast and those further inland; the former areas underwent far-reaching changes in the last two centuries BCE, with the displacement of smaller sites (generally identified as peasant farms) by larger, richer sites controlling more extensive estates, whereas inland regions were far less affected.[71] Of course, legal status is archaeologically invisible, so that 'villa' sites elsewhere in Italy (identified by their size and the quality of the remains) may well have been worked by slaves, but the logic of cost and distance implies that it would rarely have been economical to manage them intensively in the manner recommended by the agronomists. Slaves might instead have been allowed more freedom of action in managing extensive grain cultivation, or even employed rather like tenants, given responsibility for running a small farm and granted the privilege of having a family (something reserved for the overseer on the intensive villa) – but with the whole of the surplus taken by the owner, rather than just a portion. On smaller estates, a few slaves would work as assistants alongside the owner or tenant; the increased production from the additional labour inputs, on a farm large enough to support the extra workers, placed such farms in a class above the humble peasant holding worked by the family alone.

Agriculture was not the only area in which slaves were employed; they were found in all fields of economic activity, from herding (the groups of slave shepherds in the mountains, overseeing vast flocks owned by the wealthy, were notorious for their alleged criminal tendencies) to building, porterage, transport, crafts, entertainment, banking, teaching and administration, not to mention the various personal services provided for their owners.[72] Some of these jobs might not have been enthusiastically taken on by free men, but every city had a large reservoir of the unemployed – even in Rome, it was impossible to subsist on the corn dole alone – so the use of slaves must be a positive preference on the part of the owners. The same arguments apply as in the case of agriculture: slave-owning was a source of status, slaves could be forced to work harder or employed in an unusual manner without audible complaint (the tomb of the baker Eurysaces shows the different stages of bread-making and may imply a factory-like division and regulation of labour) and of course the owner took a larger profit, presumably enough to offset the original purchase price. The use of trusted slaves as agents in banking and other business, given considerable freedom of action and access to resources and offered the opportunity to accumulate wealth on their own behalf in the hope of eventually buying their freedom, suggests that the Romans preferred to rely on those who were dependent on them, both legally and personally, rather than on someone hired. One consequence of this preference was to limit the possibilities open to free men, who might get menial jobs but had little prospect of making good by working their way up in service of the rich. It was rather former slaves, freed either through purchase or through the gift of the master (most often in his will), who sometimes were able to build up their own businesses on the basis of their contacts and access to elite resources, and who left inscriptions recording both their achievements and their continuing connections to the families (and the extended *familia*) into which they had been sold. One of the great successes of the Roman slave economy was the way that it persuaded so many slaves to collaborate with their masters, including supervising and disciplining other slaves, in return for minor privileges and the hope of eventual freedom.

How far did the Romans export their model of a slave economy to the rest of the Empire? In the Greek east there was a long tradition of slave-holding, with slaves involved in personal service, craft

activity, trading and mining. There was little, besides the specifics
of the central-Italian villa system, that the Romans could teach
the Greeks about slavery. In Egypt, approximately 11% of those
recorded in census returns were slaves, a figure that is often used –
in the absence of alternative evidence – as the basis for an estimate
of the slave population of the Empire as a whole; they were more
common in towns than in villages, and assumed to have been still
more prevalent in Alexandria.[73] About one household in six listed
slaves on its census return, usually just one or two; they appear
in the papyri as scribes, cooks, barbers, other kinds of personal
servants, craftsmen and 'slaves without a trade', men-of-all-work
(e.g. *P.Oxy.* 3197; *P.Oxy.* 3510). In contrast with Italy, few seem
to have been employed as business managers or agents for their
owners, while the large estates of the wealthy, who could have
afforded to invest in the human and material capital involved in
the Roman villa system, preferred to rely on peasant labour; tied
to the land and dependent on the landowner to different degrees
but clearly distinguishable from chattel slaves.[74] When rural slaves
appear in ancient novels, they are generally working as independent
farmers rather than as part of a highly organised labour force.[75] In
this respect, at least, the demands of Rome had no obvious impact
on the organisation of production.

In the west, on the other hand, slavery was marginal before
the Roman conquest; war captives might either be kept in the
household for personal service or compelled to practice some
craft, but increasingly in the last two centuries BCE they were sold
to slave traders or merchants to fuel the slave system of Italy.[76]
There clearly was an increase in their numbers thereafter, with
large numbers known from wealthy estates in Gaul and Africa,
and the mine workers in Spain and Lusitania – an obvious case
where slaves, usually the cheapest available, could be forced to
undertake back-breaking, dirty and dangerous work.[77] Because
slavery is archaeologically invisible, leaving aside occasional finds
of iron fetters, here too there have been long debates about its
prevalence and the mode of employment in the provinces.[78] There
are only a few relevant inscriptions from the countryside recording
slave overseers, but there are few rural inscriptions of any kind, and
the overseers were the only ones likely to have an opportunity to
accumulate the money for a funeral monument.[79] The appearance of
large, well-appointed rural sites, labelled 'villas' by archaeologists,
might indeed be the end-product of several decades of successful
exploitation of slave labour in the way described by the Roman

agronomists, but it is equally possible that such estates might be worked by slaves in a less extensive manner, or might have been funded by the proceeds of some other business – representing a new form of consumption rather than of production.[80]

The strongest case can be made for southern Gaul and the coast of Spain, where traditional land-holding patterns were severely disrupted and where there is clear evidence for investment in market-orientated production of wine and olive oil; it is clear from some excavated sites, where the presence of slave quarters is almost unmistakable, that at least a minority of landowners also made extensive use of slave labour.[81] On the other hand, the passing comments of one Italian agronomist about provincial methods of training vines, which were less labour-intensive and required less specialised skills, might suggest reliance on a workforce of peasants and hired labourers rather than highly-trained slaves.[82] As suggested above, intensive exploitation of slaves was profitable in regions with easy access to a lucrative market, which would include the Mediterranean coast but not further inland, and even then it always co-existed with other forms of labour. However, even if the Romans did not export the villa mode of production to any great degree, they did export their beliefs, habits, practices and anxieties, and establish new rules of social interaction in which the display of one's dominance over others took on a particular importance. It is debatable how far the rest of the Empire became a slave economy, even if, as in Egypt, as much as 10% of the population were slaves, but it was undoubtedly a slave society and a slave culture.

INEQUALITY AND RISK

The political integration of the Roman Empire depended on connectivity, the ability to mobilise and transfer resources, and people and information; the Empire was founded on the surplus production of millions of peasant farmers, and the existing structures of trade and transport which could be used to collect and redistribute that surplus. At the same time, political integration and the various measures which the Roman state took to safeguard its dominance promoted further connectivity; so, too, did the way that the political elite spent the wealth accumulated from conquest. Imperialism created new centres of demand, which relied on the market for supplies and had the money to pay for them; it subsidised, through the construction of transport infrastructure and the lowering of transaction costs, the networks of traders and shipowners who responded to those demands; it offered incentives to producers to change their products and increase their production in order to keep the army and the cities supplied. In comparison to modern globalisation, the level of economic integration was limited by the slowness of communication and the ballast of the subsistence economy, which, even in the most monetised and market-orientated regions of the Empire, still represented the bulk of production. A city like Rome was of course heavily dependent on the products of particular regions, and news of harvest failure in Africa or Egypt affected prices and provoked panicked searches for alternative sources of supply – but the reverse was not true; Rome and Egypt were not *inter*-dependent, and there is no evidence for a political crisis in Rome, say, having any effect on Egyptian grain prices.[83] Rome remained, in Wallerstein's terms, a world-empire rather than a world-economy.[84] Nevertheless, compared with earlier periods and with comparable empires, the market sector of Rome's economy was considerable, sent into motion by the dynamics of what Michael Mann has termed the 'legionary economy' but taking on a life of its own.[85]

The result was, at the least, a dramatic increase in the volume of goods being exchanged and distributed across the Empire, and significant growth in production, as new lands were brought into cultivation or cultivated more intensively, new techniques, technology and crop varieties were diffused through the western provinces, and industrial output expanded – one of the most striking pieces of evidence for Roman economic growth is the level of atmospheric pollution, including copper residues, during this period, identified in Greenland ice cores.[86] The productivity of the land certainly increased, at least in the previously under-exploited western provinces, but it is considerably less certain whether the productivity of labour increased significantly as well. Technology was only sporadically applied in certain areas of activity, and would have had at best an incremental effect on production; the same was true of changes in the organisation of labour. Roman economic growth was extensive rather than intensive. It is equally uncertain whether the increase in total gross domestic product represented a rise in real income per head, or whether – as in other pre-industrial societies before the demographic transition – increases in production were in due course matched or exceeded by increases in population, pulling Roman society back towards the steady state.[87] The Roman elite and their collaborators commanded greater resources than ever before, but that could equally well represent greater efficiency in appropriating surplus production from its producers (not least through the use of slave labour) rather than an actual increase in the size of the Empire's overall surplus.

This raises an important point: considering economic development and growth at a global level and focusing on examples of innovation and ingenuity ignores the extent to which different sectors of society may experience such changes quite differently; globalisation and connectivity are not, contrary to the claims of their promoters, uniform in their effects, or uniformly beneficial. There was considerable regional variation, revealed above all by the archaeology of rural settlement. In Gaul, for example, the south was heavily disrupted in the late first century BCE by the confiscation and redistribution of land by Roman autocrats, whereas the north was undisturbed. Within a century, both areas had a dispersed pattern of settlement with plenty of small farms and villa sites; the south was exporting wine to Italy, and even the more isolated north was enjoying growth and prosperity.[88] In Greece, in contrast, the appearance of a few luxurious villas coincided with an overall decline in the number of rural sites; both contemporary accounts and the decline in the level of 'off-site' finds (seen as evidence for a decline in manuring) indicate that the effects of the conquest persisted long after pacification, with poverty and debt leading the poorer farmers to adopt less intensive methods of cultivation and to farm only the best land. A few well-off families seized the opportunity to build up extensive holdings, and the country began to export grain, olive oil, flax and other goods, but there is little evidence for market-orientated specialisation and none for investment in new forms of agriculture.[89] Spain suffered centuries of war, so that the coastal regions with their economic resources and easy access to markets developed well in advance of the interior.[90] Within Italy, there was wide variation in regional development, with extensive disruption and reorganisation in areas close to Rome and comparatively little change in more isolated regions. Across the Empire, as already noted, there is no sign of under-development in the modern sense, since there was no comparative advantage on which it could be based; the relationship between the centre (which in the case of Rome included the frontier provinces) and the periphery was between agrarian regions at marginally different levels of development, not between industrialised and agrarian regions.[91] However, different regions did enjoy very different fortunes, determined by a combination of the experience of Roman conquest and its aftermath, the natural resources of the region and its location in relation to major centres of demand, and networks of exchange and communication.

This variation could be characterised as the distinction between the winners and losers in Roman development – the regions that were well connected and able to take advantage of the new economic opportunities versus those that were left isolated and stagnant. Considering the level of disruption entailed by that development – the changes in rural settlement patterns in central Italy, Gaul or Greece were at least in part the product of dispossession, poverty, debt and the forcible movement of people – the value judgements could be reversed; some regions were insulated from the insidious effects of Roman globalisation, left to pursue the traditional goals of food security and satisfaction of needs rather than ever-increased profit. It is notable that those regions of Italy that were largely untouched by the emergence of the market-orientated slave villa were also less affected by a decline in rural settlement in the late first and early second century CE, apparently linked to a crisis in the market sector.[92] Isolation meant fewer opportunities for selling surplus produce, less access to the developing global culture and higher costs in importing goods; it also meant there was less risk of going hungry because local grain supplies had been bought up by merchants for export, and less exposure to the diseases that Roman connectivity could now efficiently distribute across the Mediterranean world. The bubonic plague of the sixth century CE began in ports and followed the lines of the Roman roads, and if the course of earlier epidemics like the devastating Antonine plague of the second century CE could be charted it is likely that they would have been similar.[93]

The crucial question is whether the mass of the population in less isolated regions benefited from economic development; the difficulty is, as ever, that the sources have little to say about the lives of the majority. It is clear that the idea of the entirely self-sufficient peasant family is a myth, developed in part by the Roman elite themselves; farmers always needed to dispose of some produce in order to obtain goods they could not produce themselves, and as the use of coinage became commonplace, especially in the cities, they are likely to have sold rather than bartered their surplus.[94] They would therefore be at least distantly aware of changes in demand through the impact on the prices they received for their goods, and were therefore presented with incentives to change their farming practices. They might also be compelled to do so by superior powers. Some rents and taxes continued to be collected in kind, as a portion of the total harvest, which gave no incentive to change farming practices. Where they were collected in coin, however – as they increasingly were in many regions of the Empire – producers were forced to enter the market to obtain money with which to pay, and had a clear incentive to increase their marketable surplus.[95] A wish to participate in urban social life, or to obtain the 'mass luxuries' that were becoming markers of status and necessities of everyday existence, offered a further incentive.[96] However, the capacity of many peasants to increase their production significantly was limited by the size of their holdings and the level of their resources; they could increase labour inputs, but lacked access to capital.

There is clear evidence for wealth distinctions amongst the mass of the population; some peasants, certainly, were in a position to seize market opportunities and improve their condition, above all by acquiring land holdings large enough for animals to be a worthwhile investment, so that they so benefited from both increased labour power and improved fertility.[97] A recent study of Roman Egypt suggests that the majority of its inhabitants could reasonably be described as 'sleek', basically healthy, well-nourished and prosperous, and analysis of some skeletons from Italy shows that Romans could be at the upper end of both height and nutritional status compared with other pre-industrial populations.[98] Other evidence from the same region, however, indicates the presence of a wide range of nutritional deficiencies, and supports the impression that many Romans were poorly-fed and unhealthy – which in turn would reduce their capacity to work and improve their lot.[99] The relative proportions of the prosperous and the poor in Roman society are unknown, and it must be said that there is no evidence for any overall increase in absolute poverty during the Roman period – relative poverty, and the feelings of shame and exclusion in the face of the prosperous lifestyles of others, was a different matter.[100] Equally, however, there are no grounds for supposing that the whole of the Empire benefited significantly from its economic development.

The bulk of the evidence of changes in production relates to the estates of the elite. It is perhaps only the Roman idealisation of traditional peasant values, so that an agronomist like Varro chose to present the innovations of the villa mode of cultivation as a continuation of the sort of farming practised by the Romans for centuries, that makes this seem anything other than inevitable. The Roman elite always had need of cash, to fund its political and social activities, and was willing to exploit any number of different sources of profit. They had access to capital to invest in such developments, and large enough estates to make such investment worthwhile; they could draw upon technical and scientific literature on farming, rather than relying on traditional practices, and could afford to try new methods without any risk of endangering their food security. They often controlled more than one stage of the production process, investing in processing equipment and even manufacturing storage containers like amphorae on their estates; the ideology of self-sufficiency in this case is less a matter of irrational tradition than of profit maximisation through an integrated business model, keeping direct control of costs and avoiding reliance on other suppliers. In the sale of produce, too, they enjoyed significant advantages over the peasantry: they had the capacity to store their surplus until the price was favourable, whereas smaller farms might have to sell immediately whatever the state of the market. Furthermore, they were sometimes able to transfer the costs of transport to the merchants who came to their estates to buy their produce, whereas peasant farmers had to carry their small surpluses to the market.

The rich were even able to transfer some of the risks of an uncertain climate, by selling the rights to a share of the future harvest.[101] The speculators had no legal redress if the harvest was disappointing; Pliny described how in such a situation he devised a compensation scheme, rewarding those who had invested the most in gambling on his produce and those who had paid up promptly, but it is clear that he was under no obligation to do so:

> This seemed a suitable way both of expressing my gratitude to each individual according to his past merits, and of encouraging them not only to buy from me in future but also to pay their debts... The whole district is praising the novelty of my rebate and the way in which it was carried out, and the people I classified and graded instead of measuring all with the same rod, so to speak, have departed feeling obliged to me in proportion to their honest worth.
>
> (*Letters*, 8.2.6–7)

Pliny thus personalised his relationship with regular business partners and placed them under obligation to him, which might pay off in future dealings, at the same time as enhancing his reputation in the local community; the incident stresses the disparity in the social and economic positions of landowner and merchant, which regularly gave the former an economic advantage.

At all stages in the production, distribution and consumption of goods, therefore, the landowning elite held significant advantages and claimed the bulk of the profits to be gained from supplying the new demands of Roman imperialism. Their greatest advantage was, of course, sheer scale: the large estates that would bring a steady income whether or not they invested in new approaches. This gave them the economic power to buy up the most fertile land and push peasant farms towards the margins (a process that can be seen in archaeological surveys from Greece to Italy and Gaul). However, the main source of that economic clout was the political and military power that allowed many of them to accumulate extensive properties in the provinces through seizure and dispossession, to acquire large dependent workforces, and to call upon the power of the state and the law to dominate their tenants and protect their position against other economic actors. The dynamics of Roman imperialism created economic growth, and a share of that was enjoyed by the more energetic and (probably more importantly) lucky peasants and merchants; but, intentionally or not, its main economic consequence was to give the landowning elite ever greater control of the surplus production of the Empire.

4
'They Called it "Civilisation"': The Dynamics of Cultural Change

> He began to train the sons of the chieftains in a liberal education, and to prefer the native talents of the Briton as against the trained abilities of the Gaul. As a result, the nation which used to reject the Latin language began to aspire to rhetoric; further, the wearing of our dress became a distinction, and the toga came into fashion, and little by little the Britons went astray into alluring vices: promenades, baths, sumptuous dinners. The simple natives gave the name 'civilisation' to this aspect of their slavery.
>
> (Tacitus, *Agricola*, 21)

The Roman Empire is associated above all with the bringing of 'civilisation' to the barbarians: sanitation, aqueducts, roads, irrigation, medicine, education...[1] The significance of Roman imperialism in world history, in this view, was its transformation of the culture of the provinces through the process known as 'Romanisation'; the Romans created the first truly universal culture, building on the innovations of the Greeks, and by introducing it across Europe laid the foundations for the birth of modernity and the future triumph of the West. According to the nineteenth century British historian J.R. Seeley, the reason why we should be interested in Rome – unlike most other empires, ancient or modern – was 'the superiority in civilisation of the conquerors to the conquered', so that the conquest led to positive developments in the conquered regions. Indeed, 'the effect produced upon the nations of Europe by the conquests of Rome', because of its duration and familiarity, 'stands out in the very centre of human history, and may be called the foundation of the present civilisation of mankind'.[2] Such claims have underpinned the privileged position of the classical tradition in European culture for centuries; even when modern scientific knowledge came definitively and irrevocably to supersede ancient wisdom, the classical world was still taken as the point of origin for the rationalism and spirit of enquiry that now, in the myth of modernity, was reaching its maturity. Modern writers are more likely to recognise the existence of other living cultural traditions, whereas earlier commentators saw only a confrontation between

Western civilisation and moribund Eastern culture or the primitivism of Africa and America; but for many of them, Rome remains central to the story of humanity: the source of Western superiority because other cultures have only drawn on its legacy at second-hand, or have indeed rejected many of its fundamental tenets. For example, of the five characteristics which Samuel Huntington regards as definitive of Western civilisation before the modern era, and hence as the basis for distinguishing it from all other (inferior) civilisations, three are directly linked to the influence of the Roman Empire in Europe – the classical legacy of Greek philosophy and rationalism disseminated by Rome, the influence of Latin on European languages and the rule of law inherited from the Romans – while the others were established when the Empire became Christian from the fourth century CE.[3]

The role ascribed to Rome in the foundation of Western civilisation, as both innovator and disseminator, is frequently taken as a justification for imperialism, ancient and modern. It underpins the claims of the imperial power to superiority over its subjects – not merely in military force or technology, but in its overall level of human achievement – and also justifies any action taken with respect to inferior cultures, provided that this is presented as being for their own good. Even if it begins in bloodshed, imperialism is seen to have beneficial effects on its subjects in the medium- and long-term: 'In the first instance, indeed, Roman imperialism was little more than an Imperialism of conquest, but it was a conquest that ultimately justified itself as a furtherance to civilization.'[4] This is not the problematic argument that 'might is right' found in debates about the actions of the Athenian Empire against other Greek states (Thucydides' presentation of the Melian dialogue has been enormously influential in the development of 'realist' theories of international relations, from Thomas Hobbes onwards, but it has always been controversial); rather, Roman power is seen as the product of its superior culture, so that the exercise of its might is as much a duty towards inferiors as a show of strength. This idea of the civilising mission of empire has been brought forward as a justification of their activities, with explicit reference to Rome, by the Spanish in Latin America, the French in North Africa and the Italians in Libya and Abyssinia, as well as by the British in America, India and Africa.[5] As Seeley suggested, discussing the introduction of Anglophone education into India, 'it marks the moment when we deliberately recognised that a function had devolved on us similar to that which Rome fulfilled in Europe, the greatest function which any government can ever be called upon to discharge'.[6] This did not necessarily require complete identification with the Romans; in Britain, France and Germany, some writers were equally interested in the experiences of the conquered natives whom they saw as their direct ancestors.[7] However, the crucial element of such accounts was the recognition of the need of these ancestors for the civilisation which the Romans brought, as the means to full national development, building on the foundations laid by Rome (and perhaps avoiding the vices of over-refinement that were seen to have brought down the Empire). In other words, even a nationalist narrative that regarded the Romans as foreign conquerors still perpetuated the idea that natives were capable of being raised to a higher level through contact with a superior culture. Or at any rate, some natives were; if the Indians or Africans proved more resistant to change than the ancestors of the British or French had done, that was due to their inherent flaws rather than to any problem with the idea of the civilising mission of imperialism.

This licence for intervention in cultures perceived as inferior is undoubtedly the most problematic aspect of the legacy of Roman imperialism. However, the fact that this aspect of Rome's history has been appropriated for dubious modern purposes does not automatically invalidate the account of its influence on later European culture, nor, more importantly, of the impact of the Empire on its subjects. There is widespread agreement amongst historians about the extent of the transformation of the provinces, especially in the western half of the Empire, under Roman rule. As discussed in previous chapters, there was a dramatic increase in urbanisation, both the numbers of cities and towns and the proportion of the population living in them, along with the whole array of urban institutions, infrastructure and customs – markets, temples, bathhouses, fountains, theatres and amphitheatres, aqueducts, drainage, paved streets and so forth. There were changes in diet, with the spread of a taste for refined foodstuffs like bread, wine, olive oil and fish sauce; changes in housing, both in the design of residences and in the installation of features like mosaics and bath houses; changes in religion, with the spread of cults associated with Rome (above all, cults of the emperor) and changes in local practices; changes in language, with the displacement of native languages by Latin, and in the display of language through the adoption of the 'epigraphic habit' of commemorating one's status and achievements through inscriptions; and changes in the conduct of everyday life, with the adoption of coinage, weights and measures and the law. The overwhelming impression is that the people of the Empire, over time, 'became Roman', whether through choice or coercion. The mechanisms by which this far-reaching cultural transformation was brought about have been a hotly-debated topic for decades, as will be discussed below, but there is little disagreement about the existence of a phenomenon that requires explanation.

One central issue is the nature of the relationship between political and socio-cultural structures, between cultural change and imperialism. The transformation of provincial society can be seen as the direct consequence of Roman rule, partly through the influx of Romans (soldiers, administrators, merchants and settlers) into a newly-conquered region, bringing their customs and culture with them, and partly through the active involvement of the Roman state in promoting cultural change. At the same time, however, as the passage from Tacitus makes clear, cultural change was one of the factors that made imperial rule on the Roman model possible; native people who had been 'civilised' did appear, generally speaking, to acquiesce in their rule by the Romans and to identify with the ruling power. From the perspective of the nineteenth and early twentieth centuries, one of the most striking achievements of the Roman Empire, in stark contrast to their own experiences in their overseas possessions, was its success in 'assimilating' the natives and making them into full Romans. The Roman Empire, it was believed, was far more than a structure of domination: 'Bound together not only by a common ruler, but by a highly organized and uniform though elastic system of administration, and as time went on by a common system of law and a common citizenship, it became the most powerful engine of assimilation that the world has ever seen.'[8] Particularly striking was the fact that the Romans had been able to extend full political rights to so many of their subjects: 'the Romans stood out beyond almost all peoples in the extent to which they disregarded race, and in the liberality with which they widened their citizenship'.[9] The creation of Romans out of foreigners and citizens out of subjects was the primary reason for seeing Rome as a relevant comparator for modern imperialism.

> Its imperial system, alike in its differences and similarities, lights up our own Empire, for example in India, at every turn. The methods by which Rome incorporated and denationalised and assimilated more than half its wide dominions, and the success of Rome, unintended perhaps but complete, in spreading its Graeco–

Roman culture over more than a third of Europe and a part of Africa, concern in many ways our own age and Empire.[10]

In contrast, the British experience of trying to assimilate the natives in India and Africa was judged to be an unmitigated failure.[11] Of course, it could be argued that, in some respects, the Romans had had an advantage in the nature of their conquests, since they had to deal with tribes rather than nations and with easy-going polytheism rather than 'proper' religion', and they faced comparatively few racial problems: 'the Romans were not called upon to deal with large numbers of coloured races'.[12] However, it was also seen as a matter of attitude; the Romans saw conquered natives as barbarians, undoubtedly, but barbarians capable of acquiring civilisation, whereas Europeans suffered from a basic prejudice against all other races. Roman civilisation was regarded as something that could be exported, and, more importantly, a native who had successfully adopted Roman ways could be accepted as a full member of Roman society – one simply had to list the number of leading Romans under the Principate, from a philosopher and imperial advisor like Seneca to a poet like Martial and a whole line of emperors, who came from provincial backgrounds:

> In the third century A.D. a Gaul, a Spaniard, a Pannonian, a Bithynian, a Syrian called himself a Roman, and for all practical purposes was a Roman. The interests of the Empire were his interests, its glory his glory, almost as much as if he had been born in the shadow of the Capitol. There was, therefore, no reason why his loyalty should not be trusted, no reason why he should not be chosen to lead in war, or govern in peace, men of Italian birth. So, too, the qualities which make a man capable of leading in war or administering in peace were just as likely to be found in a Gaul, or a Spaniard, or a German from the Rhine frontier as in an Italian... It is far otherwise in India, though there was among the races of India no nation. The Englishmen does not become an Indian, nor the Indian an Englishman. The Indian does not as a rule, though of course there have been not a few remarkable exceptions to the rule, possess the qualities which the English deem to be needed for leadership in war or the higher posts of administration in peace. For several reasons...he can seldom be expected to feel like an Englishman, and to have that full comprehension of the principles of British policy which may be counted on in an Englishman.[13]

The importance of these two factors, the complete cultural transformation undergone by the natives and their subsequent acceptance by the imperial power as full and equal members, is also emphasised in more recent writings on empire. The nature of empire, incorporating a wide range of different groups into a single political body, means that imperial rule is above all concerned with and dependent upon the management of diversity.[14] For Michael Doyle, the longevity of any empire – and Rome is once again his basic model – depends not only on administrative coordination but on continuing integration, passing the 'Augustan threshold' from conquest to domination and developing towards the 'Caracalla threshold' where the empire ceases to be organised around the domination of diverse groups by a single power – even if that is understood as assimilation under a common tyranny.[15] Michael Mann similarly sees a shift from a conquering empire of domination to a territorial empire, based on the integration of its subjects into the imperial system; the crucial difference is that he sees this in terms of the integration of local elites into the common culture, with changes in the culture of the mass of the population regarded, implicitly, as irrelevant to the fate of the Empire.[16] In other words, the cultural transformation of the provinces was not only Rome's greatest achievement, bringing civilisation to the barbarians, it was also the foundation of Rome's success in ruling a large and diverse area for so long.

'ROMANISATION'

The creation of a uniform world-wide civilization and of similar social and economic conditions is now going on before our eyes over the whole expanse of the civilized world. This process is complicated, and it is often difficult to clear up our minds about it. We ought therefore to keep in view that this condition in which we are living is not new, and that the ancient world also lived, for a series of centuries, a life which was uniform in culture and politics, in social and economic conditions. The modern development, in this sense, differs from the ancient only in quantity and not in quality.[17]

The term that is usually invoked in discussions of the transformation of the provinces is 'Romanisation'. This approach is closely associated with the nineteenth-century German historian Theodor Mommsen and the British archaeologist Francis Haverfield, and in the development of the discipline of ancient history their work represented a significant shift in understanding.[18] Mommsen's writings, especially his book on *The Provinces of the Roman Empire* (1885; English translation 1886), drew attention away from the political history of the Principate, which tended in the nineteenth century to be understood in a fairly superficial manner – not least as a result of overly literal readings of the classical literary sources – as a story of tyranny and decadence, and focused it instead on the fate of the rest of the Roman world. He emphasised the fact that the Empire had not only persisted for centuries after the supposedly catastrophic end of the republic and the establishment of autocracy, but had in fact brought peace and prosperity to most of its inhabitants. Furthermore, in developing this perspective both Mommsen and his admirers considered a much wider range of evidence than the literary sources and works of art on which ancient history had traditionally been based. Mommsen was best known for his work on Latin epigraphy – collecting, editing and commenting upon the inscriptions put up by thousands of provincials, and making manifest their adherence to Roman values and culture. Haverfield and other British archaeologists meanwhile turned their attention to the wealth of material evidence, not as a desperate expedient to compensate for the lack of literary sources for Roman Britain but as a means of gaining access to the experiences of a far larger proportion of the population than was usual in ancient history. While the literary sources obsessed about intrigue and social degeneracy in the city of Rome, the material evidence gave an insight into the everyday life of the provinces and revealed that the majority of the Empire's inhabitants were enjoying a wide range of new goods, different styles of housing and the delights of urban life. Metropolitan politics were a sideshow; the Empire's enlightened rule of its conquests brought about the Romanisation of its subjects.

Contrary to the image of a uniform and inexorable process of 'Romanisation' that is sometimes brought forward as a straw man in current debates, Haverfield did at times offer a fairly nuanced picture of these developments:

Romanization was, then, a complex process with complex issues. It does not mean simply that all the subjects of Rome became wholly and uniformly Roman. The world is not so monotonous as that. In it two tendencies were blended with ever-varying results. First Romanization extinguished the difference between Roman and provincial through all parts of the Empire but the east, alike in speech, in material culture, in political feeling and religion.

When the provincials called themselves Roman or when we call them Roman, the epithet is correct. Secondly, the process worked with different degrees of speed and success in different lands. It did not everywhere and at once destroy all traces of tribal or national sentiments or fashions. These remained, at least for a while and in certain regions, not in active opposition, but in latent persistence, capable of resurrection under proper conditions. In such a case the provincial had become a Roman, but he could still undergo an atavistic reversion to the ways of his forefathers.[19]

The triumph of Roman culture was not inevitable, therefore, but an ongoing struggle, in which some of the conquered peoples proved themselves more amenable to civilisation than others. Nevertheless, the effect of Roman rule in most regions was to draw the provincials into a common culture and way of life, raising them to a higher standard of living and a more refined sensibility and allowing them to participate fully in the political and social life of the Empire.

While this model of the cultural impact of Rome has held sway for decades as the theoretical basis for the study of Roman Britain and the other western provinces, in recent years serious criticisms have been made of the underlying assumptions of its creators and therefore of the way that it has shaped understanding of provincial culture. At the same time as the idea of 'Romanisation' influenced ideas about the cultural role of modern imperialism, and on occasion even influenced the policies of the imperial powers, it was itself influenced by contemporary intellectual and cultural currents.[20] Rome was read through the lens of modern imperialism as much as the modern experience was understood through comparison with Rome. The most obvious example is the tendency of many of these authors to identify with Roman culture and to take it for granted that its adoption was a progressive and desirable process.[21] In many respects, for example, Haverfield was quite insistent on the differences between Roman and British imperialism – as he remarked, Roman history 'provides few direct parallels or precedents; the wise man does not look for that in history' – but the contrast was abandoned when it came to the distinction between civilisation and barbarism:

Our civilization seems firmly set in many lands; our task is rather to spread it further and develop its good qualities than to defend its life. If war destroys it in one continent, it has other homes. But the Roman empire was the civilized world; the safety of

Rome was the safety of all civilization. Outside roared the wild chaos of barbarism.[22]

The Roman conception of civilisation, and its practical expression in the provinces, matches our own expectations, since in part our expectations have been defined by the Roman tradition of *humanitas*; the combination of cities, political and economic institutions, technology and literary heritage is precisely what modern imperial powers believe they have to offer to the rest of the world.[23] The encounter between the Romans and their conquered subjects is therefore interpreted in terms of the meeting of culture and barbarism, or even culture and non-culture; the superiority of one system is taken entirely for granted, and the Roman Empire is evaluated in terms of the degree to which different regions conformed to the Roman template. The failure of some groups or regions to Romanise adequately is regarded as the result of the deficiency of the natives, what Haverfield referred to, tellingly, as an 'atavistic' reversion to the ways of their ancestors; the same line of rhetoric applied to the failure of contemporary Indians or Africans to appreciate the benefits of European manners or knowledge. There is no consideration of alternative interpretations, such as a failure to adopt Roman manners being understood in terms of resistance, since the natives are regarded as having no culture that could be defended or valued in the face of superior Roman civilisation.[24] In the eastern provinces, in contrast, the explanation of the relative lack of change under Roman rule is simply that the Greeks and their colonies were already in possession of a culture that was recognised as superior, one of the roots of Roman (and European) civilisation, and so there was no need for them to be Romanised.

This over-valuation of Roman culture supported a tendency to identify with those who brought it to the barbarians, and hence to excuse their 'excesses' in the process of conquest and to take an overly positive view of their motives. It also meant that the issue of agency in the processes of cultural change was largely ignored. 'Romanisation' is an ambiguous term that can be understood either as a policy or as a process – as the result of a deliberate attempt by the Romans at civilising their conquests, or as the unintended result of the incorporation of a region into the political, social and economic structures of the Empire, or as some combination of the two. Many writers in this tradition saw Rome as a self-consciously civilising power, focusing on the various texts (such as the passage of Tacitus quoted above) and inscriptions which showed Roman governors and emperors intervening to promote their 'culture' in the provinces. They were generally conscious enough of the limitations of Roman power, above all the small number of Roman officials in the provinces, to recognise that Roman culture could never have been imposed wholesale on the entire Empire; rather, the role of Roman officials was to embody their culture, to begin the process of urbanisation through the foundation of colonies and development of military camps, and to provide occasional encouragement and finance. The superiority of Roman civilisation, it was assumed, was such that it would spread through the provinces through a natural process of osmosis; it was enough for the natives to be brought into contact with Romans, whether soldiers, officials, colonists or traders, to recognise their superior status and wish to imitate them.

The close connection between these assumptions and the discourses of modern imperialism, which similarly see the colonised natives as uncultured or culture-free primitives in need of civilising, and as passive consumers overwhelmed by the superior power of European civilisation, is obvious. In recent decades, these modern discourses and 'white mythologies', the means by which non-Europeans are represented as inferior and hence in need of the benevolent intervention of European powers, have been fiercely criticised by various post-colonial theories, whose arguments have also been introduced into the study of the Roman Empire.[25] Several recent studies of Romanisation have therefore adopted what might be termed a 'nativist' perspective, emphasising the equal claims to attention of pre-Roman culture – it was not intrinsically inferior to Roman civilisation, simply different – and hence insisting on the active role of the provincials in choosing to adopt Roman culture, or elements of it, for their own purposes.[26] Cultural change is not the result of a natural process of osmosis or diffusion, but rather the product of decisions made by individuals in their own interests, above all in the pursuit of social status and position. Even before a region was conquered, the consumption of Roman goods, such as wine in Gaul, might be employed by the elite (or would-be elite) as a means of differentiating themselves from the mass of the population; the significance of such goods was that they were exotic and relatively rare.[27] After the conquest, such goods became more widely available, so that more people could seek to emulate their social superiors by changing their habits of consumption. More importantly, the elite could gain significantly greater power, and access to wider networks of power, through collaboration with the Romans; the adoption and adaption of an ever wider range of Roman practices and forms was a crucial element of their strategies of negotiation and accommodation, seeking to establish themselves as acceptable partners for their new rulers while maintaining their dominant position in local society.[28] In brief, the provincials became Roman, and indeed made themselves Roman, rather than being Romanised. In due course, these new practices became embedded in provincial society – part of the expectations of normal social behaviour rather than representing a deliberate choice to embrace 'Romanness'; in other words, provincial society itself became increasingly Roman, and identification with the Empire became the norm.

The post-colonial turn in Roman history has produced a number of significant studies in recent years; unlike the 'Romanisation' approach, where the core of the theory quickly became unquestioned dogma, many of these contributions have continued to question the theoretical assumptions of the models used to interpret the ancient evidence, even those of post-colonial theory itself. The focus on provincials as agents in their own cultural transformation has, in the view of some archaeologists, led to the occlusion of the coercive aspects of the dominant Roman culture, and hence to an overly positive view of the impact of Rome. Certainly there has been little attention to the possibility of active resistance in any form other than outright rebellion; the limited penetration of some Roman practices such as house construction or Latin epigraphy into the countryside is interpreted as a function of distance from the mainstream of society, not as a deliberate rejection of Roman culture.[29] The approach remains focused on the activities of the elite; the major markers of 'Romanisation' are those associated with the wealthier members of society, in part because the traditional conception of Roman culture has tended to set the priorities for excavations and research over the last century and a half, while the reasons offered for the active participation of provincials in becoming Roman are, on the face of it, very much elite concerns. That is not to say that these accounts deliberately exclude or ignore the mass of the population, but their focus on the visible and impressive manifestations of cultural change can lead to a neglect of the possibility of discrepant experiences.[30]

The same can be said of the geographical variation; if 'Romanisation' was primarily a matter of local elites negotiating their position under the new conditions of Roman rule, it is not immediately obvious why the elites of the eastern provinces should have made far less accommodation than those in the west. Studies of Romanisation tend, with very few exceptions, to focus exclusively on the west or on individual provinces in the west, because their subject is defined in terms of significant changes in material culture and that is where the changes are visible; if, however, the question were refocused on the nature and dynamics of the encounter between Roman and provincial cultures, it would be essential to consider the divergent experiences of regions across the whole of the Empire. One crucial question is whether the divergence visible in the material record (the number of villas and inscriptions, the persistence of indigenous burial customs and so forth) is the product of variations in the intensity of exposure to Roman culture – in other words, whether the countryside becomes less 'Romanised' than the cities because its inhabitants are more isolated from exposure to Roman culture and the incentives to adopt it – or whether different groups in provincial society and different regions of the Empire were presented with quite different incentives and pressures, concealed under the homogenising term 'Romanisation'.

Some of the most far-reaching criticisms of the new orthodoxy of self-Romanising natives have indeed been based on questioning the whole concept of Romanisation; not only the dynamics of its development, but its ontological status.[31] Underpinning both the original and the modified theories is the nineteenth-century conception of a culture as an integrated system, closely related to the special qualities of the race or nation that created it, in which every aspect of life reflects as well as constitutes the whole.[32] When an object or a practice associated with Roman culture is identified in a provincial context, therefore, it is interpreted by archaeologists as either an indication of the presence of Romans or as an example of provincials adopting elements of Roman culture. However, objects have no fixed, intrinsic meaning; we actually have no way of knowing whether, for example, a Gaul drinking wine in the first century CE thought of himself as consuming a Roman drink rather than a prestigious drink, or whether mosaic decoration in a country residence was associated with Romanness by provincials to the same extent that it is by modern scholarship. Certain objects must, we may imagine, have been difficult to disassociate wholly from their origins – the toga, for example – but even then, we cannot know whether the primary motivation of a Briton wearing a toga was to assert his identity as a Roman and emulate his rulers, or rather to mark himself out from his social inferiors through a distinctive form of dress. The progressivist view that all manifestations of 'Roman' goods and practices in the provinces must represent a movement towards the wholesale adoption of Romanness may in fact conceal a wide range of different reasons for changes in material culture.

In addition, the idea of 'Roman culture', conceived as a homogeneous and clearly-defined set of social, material and intellectual practices, is itself an invention. In part, it was invented by the Romans themselves, seeking to define their own identity, from the development of a Latin literary tradition in the second century CE to the furious arguments about what it was to be Roman (or a 'proper' Roman) in the vast literary and artistic output of what is sometimes called the 'Roman cultural revolution' under Augustus.[33] There was no single model of 'being Roman' which a provincial could have imitated, even if he had full information about the debates going on in the metropolis, rather than, we might imagine, developing a partial and idiosyncratic image of what was involved from his encounters with Romans in his locality and from different media of communication like coins, literature and sculpture. Rather, the adoption of certain practices can be understood as an attempt at defining what it is to be Roman, part of an empire-wide discourse on the subject, as much as an assertion of Roman identity.[34] The different conceptions of Romanness found in different regions of the Empire were not imperfect copies of a pure Roman identity established in the centre; on the contrary, the cosmopolitan nature of the capital, drawing in influences from every corner of the Empire, meant that Roman identity was arguably a far more problematic concept there than in any individual province.[35] Looking over the Empire, there was clearly no such thing as 'Roman identity' or 'Roman culture'; better to think of multiple 'Roman identities' and 'Roman cultures', all hybrids, sharing some elements in common but with significant differences, all undergoing a constant process of development and debate.

The modern conception of Roman culture is much broader than the Romans' own definitions; inspired by the wish to look beyond the culture of the elite, it incorporates practices such as the use of *terra sigillata* pottery and coined money which were not, as far as we know, specifically associated with Roman identity by any contemporary. There is no doubt that there were significant changes in a whole range of material practices in the Roman provinces, and a tendency towards greater homogeneity of material culture in at least some regions, both phenomena that require explanation. What is in question is the assumption that they represent a progression towards 'Roman culture' and that the only explanation required is an interpretation of the nature of this progression. Interpreting the material evidence from different provinces in terms of minor variations on a single homogeneous 'Roman culture' leads to the assumption that it must be the product of a single process, rather than being the result of a number of different processes that modern scholars have interpreted as a unity. It is clear evidence of the power of the idea of the Roman Empire, bound together in and by a common culture, that the Romans sought to identify the ideas and behaviour that united (or ought to unite) its diverse inhabitants. Modern historians have been equally spellbound by the idea, to the extent of taking it for reality.[36]

PROCESSES OF CULTURAL CHANGE

Although the idea of a single empire-wide process of Romanisation has proved misleading and unhelpful, and has all too frequently involved a problematic degree of identification with the imperial power and the discourse of modern imperialism, it is possible to identify a number of processes of social and cultural change that operated, to greater or lesser degrees, in all parts of the Roman Empire, and generated the phenomena that have been gathered together under the label 'Roman culture'. The effects of these processes were highly varied, depending on, among other things, the structures of pre-conquest society in a particular area, the manner in which the region was incorporated into the Empire, the wealth of the region, its location and its degree of involvement in wider networks of trade, migration and communication. Different regions were exposed to greater or lesser degrees of external influence and stimulus; different regions and groups had different capacities for choosing how far to resist these forces and how far to participate in the opportunities they presented. Nevertheless, as it is possible to discuss the parameters of modern globalisation, identifying the forces that shape the lives of everyone on the planet to a greater or lesser degree without claiming that every experience of globalisation must be identical, so we can discuss the emergence of global cultures under the Roman Empire without implying that this was a single, simple process.

The first such process can be labelled integration, the construction of a common sense of identity and a shared world-view as a basis for the rule of the empire and its local collaborators. 'Culture' operates within society as a source of ideological power, generating the capacity to compel obedience and acquiescence through the creation and manipulation of a shared set of beliefs that sanction the existing social order.[37] Ancient elites invested heavily in the creation of meaning and the communication of official ideology through all the media available to them; it was always far cheaper to persuade people to accept their rule and believe in its essential rightness than to employ more direct and coercive methods. The aim of the Roman ideological project was not to create homogeneity and absolute conformity amongst its subjects, but to establish the empire as a higher focus of loyalty and source of communal solidarity that superseded, without necessarily destroying, their diversity. It is most visible in the products of the central power, especially in the context of the Augustan revolution; the need to legitimise the new autocratic regime led to the employment of every available medium in the city of Rome, especially literature and visual images. These were used to anchor Augustus' claims to legitimacy in a subtly revised account of the whole of Roman history and a new conception of the role, and the necessity, of the supreme ruler in bringing peace and prosperity to the empire.[38] There is considerable scope for debate about how far the 'Augustan programme' represented a coherent and directed propaganda system, rather than the result of different coin producers, artists and writers seeking to anticipate what might please the emperor, and about whether the message of these images, poems and histories was always clearly legible or received in the way it was intended by the producers. Nevertheless, the overall effect was the establishment of the set of ideas and symbols that would be employed by the Empire for centuries to come, communicated beyond the city of Rome as a means of naturalising the Roman order.[39]

> ...the nurse and parent of all other lands, elected by the gods' will in order to make heaven itself brighter, to bring scattered peoples into unity, to make manners gentle, to draw together by community of language the jarring and uncouth tongues of nearly countless nations, to give civilisation to humankind, and to become throughout all the lands the single fatherland of humanity.
> (Pliny the Elder, *Natural History*, 3.39)

Roman ideology offered a number of different images which could be read as mutually reinforcing or contradictory, according to taste. On the one hand there was an emphasis on the overwhelming power of the Empire, especially its military power, with monumental celebrations of victories and triumphs, and images of the emperor accepting homage from defeated regions like Britannia (invariably personified as female) and resting his foot on the globe appearing on coins.[40] In literature, the Empire is presented as unlimited, all-encompassing, historically unprecedented: 'Your possession is equal to what the sun can pass.'[41] New myths and genealogies gave the Romans a central place in the narrative of world history, emphasising their descent from the Trojans and the divine sanction for Roman victory and domination.[42] At the same time, however, there was also an emphasis on the civilising mission of the Empire, whose divinely-ordained task was to bring peace and impose order for the benefit of all, and to extend the benefits of civilisation to the farthest reaches of the world.[43]

Central to this aspect of Rome's image was the emergence, out of fierce internal debate, of a new conception of citizenship and of what it might mean to 'be Roman'. In place of the traditional model of an exclusive citizenship based on birthright, Rome took the unprecedented step – 'there is nothing like it in the records of all mankind', according to one Greek commentator – of opening it to the world.[44] The story that the original population of Rome was, in contrast to pure-bred Greek city-states (in theory, at any rate), a heterogeneous mix bound together by mutual interest and solidarity rather than kinship, was an essential component, legitimising the future admission of those who wished to join the commonwealth. 'In a short time a scattered and wandering multitude had become a body of citizens by mutual agreement', Cicero declared.[45] Sallust's slightly longer account emphasised the expectations of the Romans in all such situations:

> After these two peoples, different in race, unlike in speech and mode of life, were united within the same walls, they were merged into one with incredible facility, so quickly did harmony change a heterogeneous and roving band into a commonwealth.
>
> (*The War against Catiline*, 6.1–2)

Those who wished to become Roman, and who displayed sufficient conformity to Roman expectations, would be accepted, whether free-born or former slave. The question of how easy it was to gain admittance in practice – what proportion of slaves could hope to be manumitted, what level of wealth and influence was required to win a grant of citizenship – was largely irrelevant to the ideological power of this institution. What mattered was the belief that Rome had become the *patria*, the highest focus of loyalty, to all rather than to a single people:

You have caused the word Roman to be the label, not of membership in a city, but of some common nationality, and this not just one among all, but one balancing all the rest... The division which you substituted is Romans and not-Romans. To such a degree have you expanded the name of your city. Since these are the lines along which the distinction has been made, many in every city are fellow-citizens of yours no less than of their own kinsmen, though some of them have not yet seen this city.

(Aristides, *Oration*, 26.63–4)

Collective rituals for all citizens, whether those associated with the taking of the census or the formal swearing of oaths of allegiance to the emperor, emphasised their common identity, directing attention away from any differences in status between provincials and focusing it instead onto the higher authority they all obeyed.[46]

The task of uniting all the peoples of the Empire fell above all to the emperor, or to his public persona: he was the father of his people, caring for all his subjects, directing all the affairs of the Empire, personally responsible for its well-being. There is a striking image in one of Martial's poems about the games in Rome, offering a catalogue of all the different races gathered there to watch: 'These peoples speak in different voices – but then with one voice, when you are named the true father of your country' (*On the Spectacles*, 3.11–12). The emperor personified imperial power, and presented it as magnificent and all-powerful but also benevolent, generous and compassionate. His image was everywhere throughout the empire, in every city, on coins and statues and even on cakes made for sacrifice; there is some evidence that official portraits were distributed as models, to be employed by provincials who wanted to demonstrate their loyalty by erecting yet another statue, but he might also be represented in the local idiom – as a pharaoh in Egypt, for example.[47] He was the emperor of every individual city and province as much as he was the emperor of the Empire as a whole. The phenomenon of religious cult offered to the emperor is found throughout the provinces, but there was no organised Imperial Cult; rather, every city had its own cult of the emperor, with its own minor variations in rituals and festival days.[48] The birthdays of members of the imperial family, the monthly and annual birthdays of the emperor, and the birthdays and dates of accession of his predecessors structured the year; there was no single imperial calendar of festivals and other significant occasions – Augustus' birthday was the official start of the year in the province of Asia, for example, but not elsewhere – but all provincial calendars were organised around the celebration of the emperor.[49] The numerous petitions sent to him from individuals and communities with requests for his intervention or assistance make manifest the widespread belief in his power and benevolence – even if an answer could never be relied upon.[50] Meanwhile, regular reports on his great deeds circulated to every part of the Empire, to ensure that the image was maintained. The assiduity of imperial bureaucrats in promoting that image enabled it to survive the reigns of individual emperors who fell far short of the ideal, while faith in the emperor's benevolence worked to excuse the failures of the imperial bureaucracy – if a petition was not answered, or a court's decision was obviously corrupt, it could only be because the emperor was misled or kept in ignorance by his advisors.

The creation of this empire-wide ideology was not a simple top-down process. It was undoubtedly encouraged by the emperor and by many governors, who provided the models and sometimes the finance, but its implementation was mainly left to locals: the integration of the Empire into a common political culture was achieved largely through the active efforts of those who wished to become Roman rather than those who sought to create an empire of Romans. The provincial elites competed for favour by trying to guess what form of honours would be most pleasing to their rulers, gradually learning to speak the language, both literary and visual, of imperial power – a language which did of course include reference to the fate of those who showed insufficient loyalty.[51] They also furthered the development of an empire-wide elite culture through their efforts to gain power through collaboration and gain access to the higher levels of imperial authority, and through their efforts to exert ideological power over the mass of the population in order to legitimise their rule. The advent of Rome offered a range of new techniques of self-presentation and examples of how to gain the acquiescence of the masses in elite rule; above all, as discussed in an earlier chapter, the power of the city.[52] The attempts of provincial elites to establish their own dominance, as well as display their adherence to what they thought of as Roman civilisation, was a key factor in the spread of a relatively uniform urban culture through the western provinces.

The other key factor in urbanisation, and other changes in elite behaviour, was the process of differentiation: accumulating ideological power and legitimising their rule by marking themselves off from the mass of the population. This was scarcely a new phenomenon; rather, the advent of Rome increased the resources available to the aspiring notable, with access to a much wider range of prestige goods, new forms of social behaviour (for example, the extension of literary culture and education as a means of claiming higher social status) and new techniques, as well as the prestige to be gained through association and collaboration with the ruling power. In some respects, differentiation worked hand in hand with integration, fostering the development of an increasingly homogeneous elite culture. However, this was at the expense of the integration of the Empire as a whole, with wide discrepancies in power and access to power undermining any notion of the equal status of all Romans under the emperor. The establishment of a legal distinction from the early second century CE between *honestiores* and *humiliores*, the worthy and the humble, grouping together both citizens and non-citizens in each of those categories and giving different legal rights to each, simply confirmed the success of this process of differentiation; the extension of citizenship to all inhabitants of the Empire in 212 CE can be seen as acknowledgement of the degraded status of citizenship as much as a masterstroke of integration. Furthermore, the fact that 'Roman identity' was an essentially contested concept rather than a clear set of expectations and rules meant that there was continual debate (in Rome, at any rate) concerning means of social differentiation that might appear to threaten elite solidarity; the discourse concerning the acceptable limits of 'luxurious' behaviour – which shaped modern discussion of economic development for centuries – is the most obvious example, including the portrayal of the unacceptable vulgarity of the freedman Trimalchio in Petronius' *Satyricon*.[53] The meaning and acceptability of a particular practice depended, of course, on context; traditional forms of consumption in Asia Minor, for example, might appear unacceptably decadent in Rome or Gaul, while the adoption of 'Roman' practices by the Judaean elite, perfectly innocuous and commonplace in most of the Empire, undermined their legitimacy in the eyes of the population.

Whereas processes of integration were driven almost exclusively by the political elite in support of its own power, differentiation occurred much further down the social scale. The obvious problem in exploring this issue is that the consumption habits of the masses have to be reconstructed from material evidence alone, which shows how individuals were changing their practices but not why, whereas our perspective on elite behaviour comes in part from their reflections and self-presentation in literature and epigraphy.[54] However, we can reasonably assume that that consumption could be used as a means of establishing social position and membership of society, especially as citizenship no longer conferred significant political rights and duties as an alternative basis for social identity. The development of systems of distribution gave easier access to a wider range of goods, at least to those living in the cities, which could be employed as social markers; and the expansion of economic opportunities meant that at least some families had increased means at their disposal. Indeed, the process may have become self-perpetuating in the course of Rome's development into a society organised around the consumption of goods rather than collective activities; poverty became more visible because lack of resources meant an inability to imitate the practices of one's neighbours, and so there was an added incentive for those who could afford it to continue to spend to ensure that their freedom from shameful poverty and their full participation in social activities was properly advertised.[55] There is no way of knowing how far customs such as bathing, new styles of dress, new foodstuffs or the use of *terra sigillata* pottery were seen as explicitly or specifically 'Roman', nor how far ordinary provincials, unlike the literate elite, thought of themselves as Roman in ideological opposition to everyone outside the Empire. While the degree of change in the material practices of the wealthier non-elite members of provincial society is impressive, especially in the west, the consumption habits of the Empire were never completely homogeneous; for example, an analysis of meat consumption indicates that north-western regions continued to eat more beef, sheep or goat while southern Gaul and Italy remained pork-eaters, exactly as the situation before the Empire came.[56]

The society, culture and habits of consumption of the eastern provinces were, as has been noted, much less dramatically affected by the advent of Roman rule. One obvious reason is that their elites were already well established, and indeed had contributed significantly to the development of the model of elite culture and urbanism that was now extended westwards. However, they played an important role in a third process of cultural change, which can be termed re-evaluation: local customs and ideas were reviewed and revised in the face of the rise of Rome and the establishment of a more interconnected, globalised society, which brought with it a flood of new ideas and information. Writers from the Greek east thought deeply about Rome's history and its place in the grander narrative of world history, in the course of considering their own place within the new order and negotiating an accommodation with Roman power.[57] This echoed the re-evaluation of Roman history and identity that had begun in Rome itself towards the end of the republic, in response to the encounter with alien cultures and with Greek culture in particular, and the consequent anxieties over whether Roman traditions were adequate to negotiate this new world.[58] By the time of Augustus, the cultural heritage of the Greeks was becoming accepted and firmly established in Rome – in Horace's famous line, 'Captive Greece took her savage victor captive'.[59] The Greek literature of what is known as the 'Second Sophistic' developed in response to the sort of attitude expressed by Pliny in a letter to a friend who was about to take on administrative responsibilities in the province of Achaea:

> Pay regard to their antiquity, their heroic deeds, and the legends of their past. Do not detract from anyone's dignity, independence or even pride, but always bear in mind that this is the land which provided us with justice and have us laws, not after conquering us but at our own request... To deprive them of that last shadow and trace of freedom which is all that their title is, would be the harsh and wild act of a barbarian.
>
> (*Letters*, 8.24)

Greek writers established common ground with their new rulers in the dialectic of civilisation and barbarism, presenting their own nation as the originators of civilisation and treating the Romans as the agents of the diffusion of their culture to the world. A major theme in their writings is the consideration of the nature of Greek identity; almost all of them were Roman citizens, and the invention of an idea of 'Greekness' as something that could be acquired through education rather than birth ran in close parallel, and doubtless involving mutual influence, with the invention of 'Romanness'.[60] Meanwhile, many Greek cities became transformed through the construction of new buildings commemorating past greatness, some built by Roman Hellenophiles and some by local elites, into theatres of memory, reflecting and reinforcing the claims of Greece to a special place in the grand narrative of Roman power.[61]

The Greek experience of Roman rule was strikingly different from that of many other provinces, above all because of its past. Elsewhere in the Empire, the process of re-evaluation can be seen above all in the area of religious practice and ideas. The Romans chose to interpret the religions of foreign peoples in terms of their own; rather than regarding, say, the Carthaginians' Baal as an alien God, they identified him as Saturn. Caesar's description of the religion of the Gauls is typical:

> They especially worship Mercury among the gods. There are many images of him. They claim him as the inventor of all crafts, guide for all roads and journeys; they believe that he has special power over money-making and trade. After him, they worship Apollo and Mars and Jupiter and Minerva. They have roughly the same view of these deities as other peoples – that Apollo dispels sickness, that Minerva grants the principles of the arts and crafts, that Jupiter rules heaven, and that Mars controls wars.
>
> (*Gallic Wars*, 6.17)

The Romans made no attempt at exporting their own cults, which were closely tied to specific locations in Rome and its environs.[62] Roman colonies were expected to imitate metropolitan practices in such matters as the appointment and organisation of priests, and measures were taken in some provinces to reduce or remove the power and independence of sanctuaries and religious groups like the Druids; insofar as the Empire could be said to have a religious policy, it was to export the Roman concept of religion, especially its control by the political elite, rather than its content.[63] Nevertheless, there were significant changes in the location and appearance of many cult sites, with an increasing focus on temples built in the traditional Graeco–Roman style and located in the cities. This development could be seen as another manifestation of the elite's drive to control the population through the deployment of ideological power and the crystallisation of institutions in the cities, and another example of the deployment of resources and imitation of new models as a means of asserting superior status and/or Roman identity. Other developments, however, are less easy to explain in these terms; above all, changes in the content of provincial religion. To judge from the epigraphic record, some provincials worshipped Roman deities, or the traditional local deities under their Roman identification; others worshipped composite deities – Sulis Minerva of Bath, for example – or apparently hedged their bets: 'To the god Mars Lenus or Ocelo Vellaunus and to the divinity of the emperor'.[64] Another approach is found in relief carvings that show images of 'divine marriage' between a male Roman god and a native goddess; these could be seen as representing the subordination of the native tradition, if we assume the relief's creator or viewer shared the Roman view of the status of women, but it seems equally possible that the intended message was the domestication and control of the Roman by the native.[65] In either case, what is happening in such reliefs and in the 'syncretism' of Roman and native deities is the active re-evaluation and reinterpretation of each religious tradition in the light of the other. The advent of Rome brought new ideas about gods, religious practice and religious art, forcing the provincials to review their previously unquestioned traditions; not only the shifting identities of the gods they worshipped but also the changes in religious practice and the architecture of cult sites should be understood not as the unthinking adoption of the superior culture and rejection of the old ways – as it was of course understood in the 'Romanisation' tradition – but as the active reinterpretation of religion in the light of new knowledge and ideas.[66] Just as the intellectuals of the Greek east had been compelled to reconsider their cultural traditions in the light of dramatically changed circumstances, a process which we can follow in much more detail, so the inhabitants of the western provinces re-evaluated their beliefs and practices under the influence of the Empire.

This process was encouraged above all by the concentration of people and resources, and the crystallisation of religious, political and social institutions in the cities, discussed in previous chapters. Those who wished to participate in social life under the new dispensation had to travel to these urban centres, where they encountered larger numbers and a wider range of people than their ancestors had ever done. Social interaction was intensified, and increasingly anonymous and segmented; more and more encounters were with strangers rather than kin or friends, focused on business transactions, and governed by external law rather than trust. The cities were the main point of contact between the locality and the wider world, the places where provincials were most likely to encounter new ideas as well as new goods, both brought in through the increase in connectivity and movement across the Empire. This confrontation with alien practices and ways of thinking need not necessarily lead to changes in behaviour – but traditional practices and ideas were now unavoidably recognised as one lifestyle choice amongst many rather than a given. The establishment of one's social identity was now a matter of negotiation amongst different possibilities; provincials were presented with choices, and indeed with the necessity of making a choice, about who they were.

THE COSTS OF GLOBALISATION

One way of thinking about the processes of Roman globalisation is as the expansion and proliferation of networks, shared forms of social co-ordination which require the acceptance of certain standards in order to be accepted into membership.[67] The obvious example is the network of the imperial elite, which gave access to the higher levels of social, political and ideological power to those who met the standards of wealth, education, behaviour, shared literary culture and so forth needed to be accepted into membership. However, one might equally talk of the networks of Latin speakers or the users of Roman law. One of the crucial insights of this approach is that it explains the way in which, in the experience of modern globalisation and hence arguably in the Roman case, a free choice to change one's cultural practices can feel constrained. Power, in this model, operates as much through social structures and the apparently willing acquiescence of its subjects as through overt coercion. For example, in order for a member of a native elite to maintain his power in local society under the Empire, it was necessary for him to gain admittance to the network of the imperial elite, and hence to adopt the whole range of 'Roman' behaviour and culture; what appears in the record as voluntary Romanisation may have been experienced to varying degrees as Hobson's choice, unavoidable because the costs of not joining that network would have been too high. The effect was the same, the creation of an empire-wide elite bound together by a common set of attitudes and expectations, making Roman rule possible, and the spread of Roman material practices across a wide area; what this approach offers is a middle way of understanding these developments, mediating between the ideas of imposed Romanisation and the whole-hearted embrace of Roman culture by the provincials.

This approach is most interesting when it is applied not to networks that could equally be described in more traditional terms as classes or status groups but to networks defined by the use of a particular standard.[68] Roman rule, as noted previously, led to the widespread adoption of certain standards: weights and measures, coinage, law, language. The decision to embrace one of these standards was in principle entirely voluntary, but might in practice be unavoidable, if one wanted to do business or had to interact with Roman officials (who, in the western provinces, would use only Latin); the costs of being unable to communicate with those in power, or of the business falling through because of the transaction costs involved, might be too high to leave any choice. The act of adoption of these standards does not require or imply identification with them, though in time that might develop simply through the habit of use.

The adoption of a standard is not necessarily a straightforward act; it may bring with it unintended effects. Membership of a network brings an individual into contact with new information, interpretations and practices, whether that individual likes it or not. The user of Roman coinage, for example, motivated solely by its practical utility (or, in some cases, compelled by the demands of the state or his landlord for payment in cash), was as a result constantly exposed to imperial propaganda in the images on the coins; moreover, the regular use of coins or official weights emphasised and entrenched the claims to legitimacy of the ruling power, expressed through its definition and enforcement of such standards. Latin spread through the provinces for a variety of reasons, among them the demands of army service (where orders were given in Latin) and the convenience of a common language for business; it was not necessarily adopted for its own sake, or for becoming more Roman, but the usual mode of acquisition, learning the language through the traditional literary canon, exposed the learner to the Roman cultural world and, in the case of canonical authors like Virgil, to the ideology of imperialism.[69]

Over time, certain standards became ever more dominant across the Empire, replacing local practices, and their adoption became less a matter of a choice than an unavoidable necessity in order to participate in social life. This development was not only, if at all, because of the superiority of these global standards, but because they had the backing of the dominant political and economic players. Just as the development of a more homogeneous culture and a more unified set of beliefs and attitudes made ruling the empire cheaper and easier for the Romans and their collaborators, so the adoption of empire-wide standards favoured those who operated, whether in the political, social or economic spheres, at a trans-regional level. The benefits for peasant farmers from the adoption of Roman weights and measures or coins in place of local standards were marginal at best; the benefits for merchants and for the Empire itself were enormous.

Once we discard the assumption that Roman civilisation was intrinsically superior to provincial culture and hence unquestionably desirable, the increasing homogenisation and standardisation of the cultures of the Empire appears as a process whose benefits were unevenly distributed and in some cases of questionable value. 'Network power' could (and can) be experienced as quite as restrictive and tyrannical as cruder forms of coercion and control, not least because it appears to involve the free choice to accept or reject new practices in favour of old ones. Moreover, it is more insidious and pervasive than the overt manifestations of globalisation, such as the imposition of Roman rule or the articulation of an ideology of empire. Even if 'Romanisation' in its traditional sense remained for the most part a veneer, largely confined to the elite, not affecting in the least the sense of identity of the majority of provincials, nevertheless the development of standards based on sociability influenced and constricted individual freedom of action far more than the constraints of formal sovereignty. This is precisely the concern identified in Hardt and Negri's conception of 'empire': it colonises every available space, influences every discourse and is impossible to escape without setting oneself outside normal social interaction altogether. The limited technical resources of Roman imperialism meant that there were always spaces within its borders that were largely free from its influence, but the dynamic of the system, as well as the ambitions of its ideological agenda, was to extend its reach as far as possible into everyday life and thought.

Envoi:
'Decline and Fall'

If America is the new Rome, if empire lite is the new image of empire, there is a more troubling parallel with antiquity: overwhelming military superiority does not translate into security. Mastery of the known world does not confer peace of mind. America has now felt the tremor of dread that the ancient world must have known when Rome was first sacked. Then and now an imperial people has awakened to the menace of the barbarians.[1]

If, as Hardt and Negri have suggested, 'every theory of the constitution of Empire is also a theory of its decline', then one of the most important reasons for this must be their dependence on the idea of Rome as the archetypal empire. 'Decline and fall' is an intrinsic element of Rome's image in European culture, due in part to the power of Edward Gibbon's magisterial history.[2] The fact that the Empire no longer exists, at least in physical terms, has been elaborated into an enthralling and deeply satisfying narrative of triumph and disaster, grandeur and decay, power and powerlessness, which raises questions about the permanence and stability of all human creations – if not even Rome could endure, what hope for any other society? In the middle ages, of course, the answer was simple: Rome fell because that was the divinely-ordained course of history. It had been superseded by a greater power, a truly godly order, which had preserved the best elements of classical culture and set them to the task of building a kingdom of heaven rather than earth, in confident expectation of the fulfilment of God's plan.

The progressive questioning of Christian teleology from the Renaissance onwards raised more complex questions about the fate of Rome, with discussion focusing now on the natural properties of political institutions; the Republic was taken as a powerful model of constitutional organisation, while the example of the Empire supported a sense that even the most powerful states were subject to unexpected disaster. Rome offered, as always, a mirror for different aspects of the present. In the seventeenth and eighteenth centuries, for example, as well as sustaining the critique of monarchy and the advocacy of republicanism, it provided the vocabulary of luxuriousness and moral decay, and the defining narrative of their effects on society, as a basis for debates about the consequences of economic and social change.[3] Towards the end of this period, different intellectual currents converged to transform the discourse once again.[4] New historical skills and a more critical attitude towards sources placed knowledge and understanding of antiquity on an infinitely firmer foundation. The emerging disciplines of the scientific study of society suggested new ways of interpreting the past as well as the present. New ideas about the state of contemporary society raised new and pressing questions about the relationship between past and present, and the nature of historical development. The results can be seen in the subsequent course of the debate on luxury, with the contributions of David Hume, Adam Smith and other writers of the Scottish Enlightenment: the term was reinterpreted, abandoning the moral overtones of the classical texts in favour of a positive evaluation of the role of consumption in economic growth; ancient evidence was reinterpreted and qualified, questioning how far Rome's problems were really due to luxuriousness rather than, say, to the establishment of autocracy and the loss of liberty; above all, social and economic change was seen as progressive rather than as a sign of decay. In this debate as in others, Rome retained a significant role, but on very different terms; the focus of scholars was now on the differences as much as the similarities between past and present, with the sense that the modern era might be able to take a different path from that indicated by historical precedent.

Modernity was increasingly seen as an unprecedented phenomenon, free from traditional constraints and limits. Past forms of society could no longer serve as models or examples; 'we are in an entirely new condition of society', declared the French economist Jean Simone de Sismondi, while Hegel argued that 'each period has such peculiar circumstances and is such an individual situation that decisions must be made and can only be made on the basis of the period itself'.[5] However, that did not render the past irrelevant; rather, the study of history would reveal the dynamics of social development and historical change, and thus the likely course of future developments. Inevitably Rome, as the past society that most resembled the modern era in its power and sophistication, was the focus of most attention – even if it seemed to raise worrying questions about the more optimistic views of the future. Parallels were considered in particular cases for individual states, such as the French and American republics (since their institutions were based heavily on Roman models, they endured a constant anxiety that they too might fall into autocracy) or the British Empire. 'Even the forces which laid the Roman Empire low concern the modern world very nearly, more nearly indeed than do the reasons for the downfall of any other empire about which we have full knowledge', as Haverfield argued, but many writers in the 'Greater Britain' tradition insisted instead on the range of differences that rendered any apparent resemblance insignificant.[6]

Increasingly, however, Rome was compared not with individual states but with modern civilisation as a whole. 'Modernity' was conceived as an integrated unity, in which every facet of life shared in and reflected its unique and unprecedented qualities (even if the theories purporting to characterise and explain those qualities were enormously varied and largely contradictory).[7] 'Rome' came to be similarly conceived; its historical fate was then understood not as the fall of a state or the crisis of a society but as the collapse of an entire civilisation – raising questions not just about the destiny of individual nations but also about the entirety of modern civilisation, and its conviction that humanity had triumphed permanently over barbarism. Kant remarked that 'the course which the human race follows on the way to fulfilling its destiny seems to be subject to incessant interruptions, with a constant risk of reverting to the original barbarism'.[8] Most advocates of modernity proclaimed a more optimistic view: because of the achievements of modern science, technology, social organisation and geopolitical power, the future would be radically different from the present, let alone the past, and yet recognisably the same, still modern (and, as far as the economists were concerned, still capitalist) because it would represent the progressive development of modernity. Despite such claims, however, modernity was still haunted by the past against which it defined itself, and by the threat of its return.[9] Above all, it was both haunted and fascinated by the ruins of Rome.[10]

Parallels with Rome operated in a range of modes; the sense that the future might not be as bright and shining as was generally claimed could occasionally be a source of hope or satisfaction as much as a source of anxiety. A belief in the limited future of capitalism was, after all, a prerequisite for a belief in the possibility of true social revolution; Marx interpreted the symptoms of decay in contemporary society, exceeding (in his view) those horrors recorded of the later Roman Empire, as a sign that an alternative future might be coming within reach, while William Morris welcomed the possibility of a return to a pre-industrial utopia as a relief from the evils of industrial society.[11] Far more often, however, this prospect was viewed with fear or resignation, especially in the years after the First World War, as in Oswald Spengler's account of *The Decline of the West* or the gloomy outlook of the Russian émigré historian Mikhail Ivanovich Rostovtzeff:

> The evolution of the ancient world has a lesson and a warning for us. Our civilization will not last unless it be a civilization not of one class but of the masses… But the ultimate problem remains like a ghost, ever present and unlaid: Is it possible to extend a higher civilization to the lower classes without debasing its standards and diluting its quality to the vanishing point? Is not every civilization bound to decay as soon as it begins to penetrate the masses?[12]

These discussions could take a more positive or at any rate activist turn. Occasionally, parallels with Rome were employed to suggest how people might survive the coming disaster; most recently in the proposal of Morris Berman for a 'new monasticism' to preserve the finest products of Western culture from the spiritual anomie and socio-economic breakdown of modern America: 'While the parallels between the Roman case and the American one are not exact, the analogy does suggest some transformative possibilities. If, for example, we are indeed slated for another dark age, it may not have to last six hundred years this time around.'[13] More often, the comparison is invoked by those with a firm conviction that they understand the nature of the threat to modern society as a means of bolstering their arguments, validating their views and supporting their call for specific action to preserve Western civilisation (or the United States, which is frequently assumed to be the same thing).

A wide range of lessons have been drawn from Rome's decline and fall. One of the most prominent is the need to deal effectively with the barbarians at the gates, a popular theme both among French writers in the first half of the twentieth century, confronted by the self-proclaimed successors of the Germanic hordes that had conquered Rome ('Roman civilization did not die a natural death; it was assassinated', in the words of one French historian) and among the cheerleaders of United States power over the last decade ('Modern high-tech terrorists are the new barbarians').[14] However, Rome's fall has also been blamed on excessive bureaucracy, the stifling of freedom and free enterprise by over-regulation and the unendurable weight of taxation – and on the weakness of the central state and its shortage of resources.[15] It has been attributed to a shortage of manpower and to over-population, to 'race suicide', with the pure blood of the original Romans diluted and overwhelmed by weak-willed, emotional Orientals – and to the failure of the Romans to extend their civilisation far enough amongst its subjects.[16] Various Enlightenment rationalists blamed Christianity and its effect on the civic spirit of the aristocracy; Josef Stalin firmly asserted that Rome had been brought down by the revolt of the slaves.[17] It might seem that modern preconceptions and ideological assumptions are simply being read into the past, but in fact almost all of these themes – albeit not expressed in precisely these terms – can be identified in the analyses of social crisis developed by authors at the time. Modern preconceptions and ideological assumptions merely determine the selection of particular classical views as providing the true explanation of their civilisation's problems.

One of the major problems in studying ancient authors' accounts of 'decline and fall', and hence in drawing parallels between ancient and modern, is that for many of them the Empire was always already in decline.[18] Writers of the late Republic, faced with a crisis of their political system and the social and economic consequences of empire, mourned the loss of the virtue and frugality of their ancestors and denounced contemporary tendencies to neglect tradition. The efforts of the new Augustan regime to present innovation as tradition and revolution as restoration were riddled with doubts and inconsistencies – Virgil and Livy seem to raise questions about the official line even as they promulgate it in their works – and plenty of authors of the early Principate mourned the loss of the liberty of the Republic and saw the corruption and luxuriousness of their own society as presaging the end of Rome. A long Christian tradition, building on Jewish precedents, emphasised the flaws of the Empire and of the whole worldly order as an argument for the need for spiritual renewal and a new view of the relations between god and man. Traditionalist authors of the fourth century blamed it all on Constantine's rejection of everything that Rome stood for by converting to Christianity. At all these periods, it should be noted, there were also plenty of sources proclaiming the happiness of the times and the magnificence of the empire.[19]

A full account of the history of the later Roman Empire and of the characteristics of the period known as 'late antiquity' far exceeds the scope of this book. It is a rich and complex subject, which is no longer interpreted solely in terms of the decadence of the classical and the collapse of civilisation into the Dark Ages – and as such it is almost entirely irrelevant to the use of the image of Rome in modern discourse. Arguments about whether the period might be better conceived as a transition from one form of society to another count for nothing in the face of the power of the image of 'decline and fall' in the Western imagination. That image is vague in the extreme; there is little precision, and little sense of any necessity for precision, in defining *what* is supposed to have declined and fallen *when*. By the traditional end date of 476 CE, the power of the Roman emperor in the west had long been negligible; it would have made little difference if the line had been broken decades earlier or persisted for another century, if not for the loss of the irony that the last emperor of Rome, Romulus Augustulus, carried the name of its founder and the diminutive of its first emperor. Meanwhile, the Roman Empire actually maintained its power more or less undiminished for centuries afterwards in the wealthy eastern half of the Mediterranean; only the power of the Roman church, ignorance of the Greek language, sheer insularity and general prejudice against the east persuaded anyone otherwise. Furthermore, this line of argument carries with it the assumption that 'Rome' should be understood simply in terms of its political organisation at the highest level, so that the end of the lines of emperors (in the west) must mark the end of everything. If one considers the economic, social or cultural structures of the Empire, let alone the life of the countryside, then the chronology of change appears very different, and in many cases much less dramatic than the images of catastrophic collapse. Nevertheless, the idea of 'decline and fall', resulting from some combination of external barbarians and internal weakness, and dominated by images of destruction, slaughter and the collapse of civilisation, continues to haunt the Western imagination.

At the heart of the problem is the ambiguous relation of the Roman Empire to Roman culture; this is rarely defined or clarified in modern discourse, not least because blurring the distinction between the power of a polity (deliberate, coercive) and the nebulous, inoffensive power of culture is a crucial element in the repertoire of imperialism. Culture is seen as natural, and hence stable; cultural change therefore requires explanation. Empire is thought of as unnatural, and hence inherently unstable; the real question, historians from Gibbon onwards have asserted, is not why Rome fell but how it succeeded in enduring for so long. The fate of the Roman political order, which did indeed come to an end in the west in the fifth century, is projected onto the whole of Roman culture, so that cultural change is interpreted as cultural collapse. All evidence of disruption and change in every area of life is accumulated to demonstrate the severity of the catastrophe; evidence of continuity or of a lack of drama – for example, the fact that the vast hordes of barbarians overwhelming the Empire numbered at the most a few hundred thousand, facing a population of 60 million or so – is discounted in the face of the assertion that, like it or not, the Empire did cease to exist.

In the modern discourse, the conflation of empire and culture serves to compel assent to the former – opposition to Western hegemony is presented as opposition to freedom, democracy, Shakespeare and so forth – but it also creates the impression that 'our' culture is under serious threat from the forces that threaten the empire, and demands acquiescence in whatever measures are deemed necessary to protect them. The pervasive analogy with Rome, and the dominance of the theme of 'decline and fall' in Rome's image, means that we are presented with Hobson's choice: this civilisation, warts and all, or barbarism and darkness. There is no realistic alternative; the historical record makes that clear.

> Men make their own history, but they do not make it just of their own free will; not under circumstances chosen by themselves, but under circumstances directly encountered, given and handed down. The tradition of all the dead generations weighs like a nightmare on the brains of the living. And if they nevertheless seem engaged in revolutionising themselves and things, in creating something that has not yet existed, precisely in such periods of revolutionary crisis they fearfully conjure up the spirits of the past to their service, borrow from them names, battle cries and costumes, in order to present the new scene of world-history in this time-honoured clothing and with this borrowed language. Thus Luther masked himself as the Apostle Paul, the Revolution of 1789 to 1814 draped itself alternately as the Roman republic and the Roman empire, and the Revolution of 1848 knew nothing better than to parody, now 1789, now the revolutionary tradition of 1793–5.[20]

Karl Marx's essay, *The Eighteenth Brumaire of Louis Bonaparte*, remains one of the most important and insightful discussions of the power and pitfalls of drawing on the past. On the one hand, historical examples can be a source of inspiration and courage, 'magnifying the given task in imagination rather than fleeing from its solution in reality'; analogies with Rome not only sustained the extension of Western imperial power across the globe, they also inspired the radical political traditions that opposed such brutality and oppression, not least through Marx's own reflections upon ancient history. On the other hand, history offers the illusion that we can fully understand human nature and the possibilities open to human society on the basis of our knowledge of the past, and that illusion tends to work as a conservative force, undermining any revolutionary hopes. 'The historical record shows' that revolutions always betray their ideals; 'the historical record shows' that human nature is incapable of setting aside self-interest. 'The historical record' shows that Rome collapsed into barbarism (of course, historians of early medieval Europe tend to resent the label 'Dark Ages', and insist on the vibrancy and vitality of that society, but the image of 'decline and fall' is too strong in Western culture for that to have much effect), and so we must work to preserve the existing order for fear of the alternative. The possibility of a different, historically-unprecedented development arising out of the dissolution of the present state of things is simply ignored. The power of Rome continues to compel obedience to the empire.

Modern revolution, Marx argued, 'cannot draw its poetry from the past, but only from the future. It cannot begin with itself before it has cast off every superstition about the past.'[21] The task of the historian is to understand Rome and its continuing influence in order to break its power over the modern imagination.

Further Reading

GENERAL HISTORIES OF ROME

A great many narrative accounts of the rise of Rome have appeared in recent years, as part of a general upsurge in interest in the wake of the film *Gladiator* and the television series *Rome*; most of them are perfectly serviceable, but especially recommended is N. Faulkner, *Rome: empire of the eagles, 753 BC – AD 476* (London: Longman, 2008), for its explicitly left-wing perspective and avoidance of excessive glorification of military conquest. Analytical accounts – with the exception of C. Kelly's brisk and highly readable *The Roman Empire: a very short introduction* (Oxford: Oxford University Press, 2006) – tend to follow the traditional political division between Republic and Principate, rather than considering Rome as a whole. On the earlier period, M. Beard & M. Crawford, *Rome in the Late Republic* (2nd edn) (London: Duckworth, 2000) remains a classic, even now that most of its insights have been absorbed into the mainstream of historical thought. Two recent collections draw together current ideas and debates: H. Flower (ed.), *The Cambridge Companion to the Roman Republic* (Cambridge: Cambridge University Press, 2004) and the more compendious *Companion to the Roman Republic*, edited by N. Rosenstein & R. Morstein-Marx (Oxford: Blackwell, 2006). On the Principate, P. Garnsey & R. Saller, *The Roman Empire: economy, society, culture* (London: Duckworth, 1987) is still well worth reading, along with R. Alston, *Aspects of Roman History, AD 14–117* (London & New York: Routledge, 1998).

IMPERIALISM AND IMPERIAL RULE

The most detailed study of Roman imperialism remains W.V. Harris, *War and Imperialism in Republican Rome 327–70 BC* (Oxford: Oxford University Press, 1979). C. Champion (ed.), *Roman Imperialism: readings and sources* (Oxford & Malden: Blackwell, 2004) offers an invaluable mixture of important scholarly articles, extracts from books and ancient sources. A. Lintott, *Imperium Romanum: politics and administration* (London & New York: Routledge, 1993) provides a detailed survey of the administrative structures of the Roman empire. S.E. Alcock et al. (eds), *Empires: perspectives from archaeology and history* (Cambridge: Cambridge University Press, 2001) includes a range of stimulating articles about different aspects of different pre-industrial empires. Important works on individual provinces and their development under Roman rule, especially drawing on archaeological evidence, are S.E. Alcock, *Graecia Capta: the landscapes of Roman Greece* (Cambridge: Cambridge University Press, 1993); M. Millett, *The Romanization of Britain: an essay in archaeological interpretation* (Cambridge: Cambridge University Press, 1990); G. Woolf, *Becoming Roman: the origins of provincial civilization in Gaul* (Cambridge: Cambridge University Press , 1998); D.J. Mattingly, *An Imperial Possession: Britain in the Roman Empire, 54 BC – AD 409* (London: Penguin, 2007).

ECONOMY

There is, unfortunately, no handy introduction to the nature and workings of the Roman economy; the relevant sections in Garnsey & Saller, *The Roman Empire*, remain the clearest and most accessible summary, while Chapter 2 in N. Morley, *Theories, Models and Concepts in Ancient History* (London & New York: Routledge, 2004) explores the underlying issues in the debate. M.I. Finley, *The Ancient Economy* (Berkeley & Los Angeles: University of California Press, 3rd edn, 1999) is highly readable and provocative, but Finley's view of antiquity has been increasingly questioned in recent years (as the useful introduction to this edition by Ian Morris makes clear), and he treats Greece and Rome as a unity. The latest academic thinking on the development of the ancient economy can be found in the monumental and expensive *Cambridge Economic History of Greco-Roman Antiquity*, edited by W. Scheidel, I. Morris & R. Saller (Cambridge: Cambridge University Press, 2007). Some useful articles are collected in W. Scheidel & S. von Reden (eds), *The Ancient Economy* (Edinburgh: Edinburgh University Press, 2002).

CULTURE

R. Hingley, *Globalizaing Roman Culture: unity, diversity and empire* (London & New York, 2005), summarises the key debates and offers a wealth of stimulating material and perspectives; his earlier work, *Roman Officers and English Gentlemen: the imperial origins of Roman archaeology* (London & New York: Routledge, 2000). Important collections of articles on 'Romanization' are J. Webster & N. Cooper (eds), *Roman imperialism: post-colonial perspectives* (Leicester: Leicester Archaeology Monographs, 1996), D.W. Mattingly (ed.), *Dialogues in Roman Imperialism: power, discourse, and discrepant experience in the Roman Empire* (Portsmouth, RI: *Journal of Roman Archaeology*, Supplementary Series 23, 1997) and S. Keay & N. Terrenato (eds), *Italy and the West: comparative issues in Romanization* (Oxford: Oxbow, 2001). On religion, see M. Beard, J. North & S. Price, *Religions of Rome* (Cambridge: Cambridge University Press, 1998) and J. Rüpke, *Religion of the Romans* (Cambridge: Polity, 2007). On the Greek experience and the Second Sophistic, see S. Swain, *Hellenism and Empire: language, classicism and power in the Greek world, AD 50–250* (Oxford: Oxford University Press, 1996) and T. Whitmarsh, *Greek Literature and the Roman Empire: the politics of imitation* (Oxford: Oxford University Press, 2001).

THE WORLD OF LATE ANTIQUITY

Once again, there is a wide choice of reading for this vast topic. Good narrative accounts – covering slightly different time-spans, and so placing different emphasis on the degree of continuity of change – include A. Cameron, *The Later Roman Empire* (London: Fontana, 1993), R. Collins, *Early Medieval Europe 300–1000* (2nd edn) (Basingstoke: Macmillan, 1999) and S. Mitchell, *A History of the Later Roman Empire AD 284–641* (Oxford & Malden: Wiley-Blackwell, 2006). Recommended theoretical and analytical works are A. Cameron, *The Mediterranean World in Late Antiquity* (London & New York: Routledge, 1993), P. Garnsey & C. Humfress, *The Evolution of the Late Antique World* (Cambridge: Orchard Academic, 2001) and C. Wickham, *The Inheritance of Rome: a history of Europe from 400 to 1000*

(London: Allen Lane, 2009). Two stimulating essays on the nature of the changes in late antiquity are P. Anderson, *Passages from Antiquity to Feudalism* (London: Verso, 1974) and A. Schiavone, *The End of the Past: ancient Rome and the modern west* (Cambridge, MA: Harvard University Press, 2000).

THE LEGACY OF ROME

The study of the 'reception' of classical antiquity is a relatively new area of study, with a lot of exciting work but few accessible, non-specialised introductions. L. Hardwick & C. Stray (eds), *A Companion to Classical Receptions* (Oxford & Malden: Wiley-Blackwell, 2007) focuses on the reception of different literary authors and art, while C. Martindale & R.F. Thomas (eds), *Classics and the Uses of Reception* (Oxford & Malden: Blackwell, 2006) considers the theoretical issues. On the reception of Rome, see N. Vance, *The Victorians and Ancient Rome* (Oxford: Blackwell, 1997) and the papers in C. Edwards (ed.), *Roman Presences: receptions of Rome in European culture, 1789–1945* (Cambridge: Cambridge University Press, 1999). On the reception of Rome in the United States, M. Malamud, *Ancient Roman and Modern America* (Oxford & Malden: Wiley-Blackwell, 2009). Broader conceptions of 'antiquity' and 'modernity' in the long nineteenth century are discussed in N. Morley, *Antiquity and Modernity* (Oxford & Malden: Wiley-Blackwell, 2008).

For further discussions of the Roman Empire and its legacy, go to:
www.romanimperialism.com

Notes

INTRODUCTION

1. Wyke, M., *Projecting the Past: ancient Rome, cinema and history* (London & New York: Routledge, 1997).
2. Edwards, C. (ed.), *Roman Presences: receptions of Rome in European culture, 1789–1945* (Cambridge: Cambridge University Press, 1999).
3. Marx, K. & Engels, F., *Manifest der Kommunistischen Partei* [1848], in *Marx-Engels Werke* Vol. 4 (Berlin: Dietz, 1964), p. 465. Generally on this theme, N. Morley, *Antiquity and Modernity* (Oxford & Malden: Wiley–Blackwell, 2008).
4. Folz, R., *The Concept of Empire in Western Europe* (London: Edward Arnold, 1969).
5. Moreland, J., 'The Carolingian empire: Rome reborn?', in Alcock, S.E., et al. (eds), *Empire: perspectives from archaeology and history* (Cambridge: Cambridge University Press, 2001), pp. 392–418.
6. cf. Zanker, P., *The Power of Images in the Ages of Augustus*, trans. Shapiro, A. (Ann Arbor: University of Michigan Press, 1988) and Scobie, A., *Hitler's State Architecture: the impact of classical antiquity* (University Park, PA: Pennsylvania State University Press, 1990).
7. Howe, S., *Empire: a very short introduction* (Oxford: Oxford University Press, 2002), p. 41.
8. Bryce, J., *The Ancient Roman Empire and the British Empire in India* (Oxford: Oxford University Press, 1914), pp. 6–7.
9. Pitts, J., *A Turn to Empire: the rise of imperial liberalism in Britain and France* (Princeton & Oxford: Princeton University Press, 2005), pp. 87, 236. On Ireland, see also Armitage, D. (ed.), *Theories of Empire, 1450–1800* (Aldershot & Burlington, 1998), pp. 192–4.
10. Seeley, J.R., *The Expansion of England* (London: Macmillan, 1883), p. 261; Bell, D., 'From ancient to modern in Victorian imperial thought', *Historical Journal*, 2006 (49), pp. 735–59.
11. Baring, E., Earl of Cromer, *Ancient and Modern Imperialism* [1910] (Honolulu: University Press of the Pacific, 2001), p. 127.
12. Bryce, *Ancient Roman Empire*, p. 64.
13. Bell, 'From ancient to modern', pp. 737–8; Morley, *Antiquity and Modernity*, pp. 117–40. See e.g. Robertson, J.M., *Patriotism and Empire* (London: Grant Richards, 1899) for a belief in the possibility of England escaping the fate of Rome – although agriculture is already starting to be neglected and imports beginning to exceed exports, both signs of the parasitism that brought down Rome.
14. Vance, N., *The Victorians and Ancient Rome* (Oxford: Blackwell, 1997), pp. 222–46.
15. On the decline of historical exemplarity, Koselleck, R., *Futures Past: on the semantics of historical time*, trans. Tribe, K. (New York: Columbia University Press, 2004), pp. 26–42.

16. Summarised in Mommsen, W.J., *Theories of Imperialism*, trans. Falla, P.S. (London: Weidenfeld & Nicolson, 1981).
17. *Imperialism and World Economy* (London: Bookmarks, 2003), p. 119; on Marx's approach to this question, Morley, N., 'Marx and the failure of antiquity', *Helios*, 1999 (26), pp. 151–64.
18. McCarthy, G.E., *Marx and the Ancients: classical ethics, social justice and nineteenth-century political economy* (Savage, MD: Rowman & Littlefield, 1990).
19. Speech at the anniversary of the *People's Paper*, in *Collected Works* XIV (London: Lawrence & Wishart, 1980).
20. Hobson, J.A., *Imperialism: a study* (London: Allen & Unwin, 1902), pp. 367–8.
21. Unnamed advisor to George W. Bush, cited by Ron Suskind, 'Faith, certainty and the Presidency of George W. Bush', *New York Times Magazine*, 17 October 2004.
22. See generally Malamud, M., *Ancient Rome and Modern America* (Oxford & Malden: Wiley-Blackwell, 2009).
23. Ugarte, M., *The Destiny of a Continent* [1925], reprinted in Merrill, D. & Paterson, T.G. (eds), *Major Problems in American Foreign Relations Vol. II: since 1914* (5th edn) (Boston & New York: Houghton Mifflin, 2000), pp. 84–5.
24. Noted even by one of the writers arguing strongly for a powerful, self-conscious American imperialism: Ferguson, N., *Colossus: the price of America's empire* (London: Penguin, 2004), p. 14. Generally, see Mooers, C., 'Nostalgia for empire: revising imperial history for American power', in Mooers (ed.), *The New Imperialists: ideologies of empire* (Oxford: Oneworld, 2006), pp. 111–35.
25. Nye Jr, R.S., *Soft Power: the means to success in world politics* (New York: World Affairs, 2004), p. 135; discussed by T. Mirrlees, 'American soft power, or, American cultural imperialism?', in Mooers (ed.), *The New Imperialism*, pp. 199–227.
26. Thayer, B.A., 'The case for the American empire', in Layne, C. & Thayer, B.A., *American Empire: a debate* (New York & London: Routledge, 2007), pp. 1–50.
27. Bender, P., 'The New Rome', in Bacevich, A.J. (ed.), *The Imperial Tense: prospects and problems of American empire* (Chicago, IL: Ivan R. Dee, 2003), pp. 81–92; quote from p. 83.
28. Ignatieff, M., *Empire Lite: nation-building in Bosnia, Kosovo and Afghanistan* (London: Vintage, 2003), p. 1.
29. Nye, *Soft Power*, p. x.
30. Walker, M., 'An empire unlike any other', in Bacevich (ed.), *Imperial Tense*, pp. 134–45; quote from p. 137.
31. Ferguson, *Colossus*, p. 34.
32. e.g. Lal, D., *In Praise of Empires: globalisation and order* (New York & Basingstoke: Palgrave Macmillan, 2004).
33. A Google search for "eu roman empire" turns up any number of fascinating websites on this theme. Boris Johnson's frequent contemporary allusions in *The Dream of Rome* (London: HarperCollins, 2007), including those to the European Union, are considerably more nuanced.
34. (Cambridge, MA: Harvard University Press, 2000).
35. Fisk, R., *The Age of the Warrior: selected writings* (London: Fourth Estate, 2008), pp. 368–71.

36. Quoted in Vance, *Victorians and Ancient Rome*, p. 231.

37. Mattingly, D.W. (ed.), *Dialogues in Roman Imperialism: power, discourse, and discrepant experience in the Roman Empire* (Portsmouth, RI: *Journal of Roman Archaeology* Supplementary Series 23, 1997); Hingley, R., *Roman Officers and English Gentlemen: the imperial origins of Roman archaeology* (London & New York: Routledge, 2000); Hingley, R., *Globalizing Roman Culture: unity, diversity and empire* (London & New York: Routledge, 2005).

38. Woolf, G., 'Inventing empire in ancient Rome', in Alcock, S.E., et al. (eds), *Empires*, pp. 311–22.

39. Webster, J. & Cooper, N. (eds), *Roman imperialism: post-colonial perspectives* (Leicester: Leicester Archaeology Monographs, 1996); Hardwick, L. & Gillespie, C. (eds), *Classics in Post-Colonial Worlds* (Oxford: Oxford University Press, 2007).

40. e.g. Huntington, S.P., *The Clash of Civilizations and the Remaking of World Order* (New York: Simon & Schuster, 1996).

41. On this passage, and other prophecies in the *Aeneid* about Roman greatness, see Zetzel, J.E.G., 'Rome and its traditions', in Martindale, C. (ed.), *The Cambridge Companion to Virgil* (Cambridge: Cambridge University Press, 1997), pp. 188–203.

CHAPTER 1

1. History of the Punic wars: clear summary by Gargola, D.A., 'Mediterranean empire (264–134)', in Rosenstein, N. & Morstein-Marx, R. (eds), *A Companion to the Roman Republic* (Malden & Oxford: Blackwell, 2006), pp. 147–66; more detailed accounts in Goldsworthy, A., *The Punic Wars* (London: Cassell, 2000); Hoyos, B.D., *Unplanned Wars: the origins of the First and Second Punic Wars* (Berlin & New York: de Gruyter, 1998); Lazenby, J.F., *Hannibal's War* (Warminster: Aris & Phillips, 1978). On the history of Carthage, Lancel, S., *Carthage: a history*, trans. Neill, A. (Oxford: Blackwell, 1995).

2. Ridley, R.T., 'To be taken with a pinch of salt: the destruction of Carthage', *Classical Philology*, 1986 (81), pp. 140–6.

3. For general discussions of 'Roman imperialism', see Garnsey, P.D.A. & Whittaker, C.R., 'Introduction', in Garnsey & Whittaker (eds), *Imperialism in the Ancient World* (Cambridge: Cambridge Philological Society, 1976), pp. 1–6; Champion, C.B. & Eckstein, A.M., 'Introduction: the study of Roman imperialism', in Champion (ed.), *Roman Imperialism: readings and sources* (Malden & Oxford: Blackwell, 2004), pp. 1–10; Eckstein, A.M., 'Conceptualising Roman imperial expansion under the republic: an introduction', in Rosenstein & Morstein-Marx, *Companion to the Roman Republic*, pp. 567–89.

4. Brunt, P.A., 'Laus imperii', in Garnsey & Whittaker, *Imperialism in the Ancient World*, pp. 159–91.

5. For a summary and critique of defensive imperialism, Harris, W.V., *War and Imperialism in Republican Rome 327–70 BC* (Oxford: Oxford University Press, 1979), pp. 163–54.

6. de Sepulveda, Gines, (1550) and de Vitoria, Francisco, (1539), cited and discussed by Lupher, D.A., *Romans in a New World: classical models in sixteenth-century Spanish America* (Ann Arbor: University of Michigan Press, 2003).

7. Baring, E., Earl of Cromer, *Ancient and Modern Imperialism* [1910] (Honolulu: University Press of the Pacific, 2001), pp. 19–20.

8. For example, the term does not appear in the index of Flower, H. (ed.), *The Cambridge Companion to the Roman Republic* (Cambridge: Cambridge University Press, 2004).

9. Morley, N., *Theories, Models and Concepts in Ancient History* (New York & London: Routledge, 2004).

10. Frank, T., *Roman Imperialism* (New York: Macmillan, 1914), pp. 120–1.

11. See generally Betts, R.F., 'The allusion to Rome in British imperialist thought of the late nineteenth and early twentieth centuries', *Victorian Studies*, 1971 (15), pp. 149–59.

12. Lucas, C.P., *Greater Rome and Greater Britain* (Oxford: Oxford University Press, 1912), p. 59.

13. Bukharin, N., *Imperialism and World Economy* [1915] (London: Bookmarks, 2003), pp. 118–19.

14. Ibid., p. 119. Generally on Marxist approaches, Brewer, A., *Marxist Theories of Imperialism: a critical survey* (2nd edn) (London & New York: Routledge, 1990).

15. See generally Kemp, T., *Theories of Imperialism* (London: Dennis Dobson, 1967).

16. cf. Scheidel, W., 'Sex and empire: a Darwinian perspective', in Morris, I. & Scheidel, W. (eds), *The Dynamics of Ancient Empires* (Oxford: Oxford University Press, 2009), pp. 255–324.

17. Lenin, V.I., *Imperialism, the Highest State of Capitalism* (Peking: Foreign Languages Press, 1970), p. 97.

18. See generally Rosenstein & Morstein-Marx, *Companion to the Roman Republic*.

19. Whitmarsh, T., *Greek Literature and the Roman Empire* (Oxford: Oxford University Press, 2001), and further discussion in Ch. 4 below.

20. See above, all the discussions in North, J.A., 'The development of Roman imperialism', *Journal of Roman Studies*, 1981 (71), pp. 1–9, and Rich, J., 'Fear, greed and glory: the causes of Roman war-making in the middle Republic', in Rich, J. & Shipley, G. (eds), *War and Society in the Roman World* (New York & London: Routledge, 1993), pp. 38–68; more generally, Reynolds, C., *Modes of Imperialism* (Oxford: Oxford University Press, 1981), pp. 124–71.

21. Wiseman, T.P., *Roman Drama and Roman History* (Exeter: Exeter University Press, 1998).

22. Raaflaub, K., 'Born to be wolves? Origins of Roman imperialism', in Wallace, R.W. & Harris, E.M. (eds), *Transitions to Empire: essays in Greco-Roman history 360–146 BC* (Norman, OK: University of Oklahoma Press, 1996), pp. 271–314.

23. Harris, *War and Imperialism*, pp. 54–130.

24. Richardson, J., *Hispaniae: Spain and the development of Roman imperialism, 218–82 BC* (Cambridge: Cambridge University Press, 1986).

25. North, 'Development of Roman imperialism'.

26. Polybius, 32.13.7–9.

27. Eckstein, 'Conceptualising', pp. 570–1.

28. See further Ch. 3 below.

29. On the *publicani*, Badian, E., *Publicans and Sinners: private enterprise in the service of the Roman Republic* (Ithaca, NY: Cornell University Press, 1972).
30. Harris, *War and Imperialism*, pp. 9–53.
31. Beard, M., *The Roman Triumph* (Cambridge, MA: Harvard University Press, 2007).
32. e.g. Loomba, A., *Colonialism/Postcolonialism* (London & New York: Routledge, 1998), pp. 5–10; Bush, B., *Imperialism and Postcolonialism* (Harlow: Pearson, 2006), pp. 48–50.
33. Robinson, R., 'Non-European foundations of European imperialism: sketch for a theory of collaboration', in Owen, R. & Sutcliffe, R. (eds), *Studies in the Theory of Imperialism* (London: Longman, 1972), pp. 117–40; discussed by Mommsen, W.J., *Theories of Imperialism*, trans. Falla, P.S. (London: Weidenfeld & Nicolson, 1981), pp. 70–112.
34. cf. Mommsen, W.J., 'The end of empire and the continuity of imperialism', in Mommsen, W.J. & Osterhammel, J. (eds), *Imperialism and After: continuities and discontinuities* (London: Allen & Unwin, 1986), pp. 333–58.
35. Doyle, *Empires*, pp. 88–92; Eckstein, 'Conceptualising'.
36. How, W.W. & Leigh, H.D., *A History of Rome to the Death of Caesar* (London, New York & Bombay: Longmans, Green & Co., 1896), p. 235.
37. e.g. Bender, P., 'The New Rome', in Bacevich, A.J. (ed.), *The Imperial Tense: prospects and problems of American empire* (Chicago, IL: Ivan R. Dee, 2003), pp. 81–92; Ferguson, N., *Colossus: the price of America's empire* (London: Penguin, 2004); Lal, D., *In Praise of Empire: globalization and order* (New York & Basingstoke: Palgrave Macmillan, 2004). For a critique of such arguments, see Mooers, C., 'Nostalgia for empire: revising imperial history for American power', in Mooers, C. (ed.), *The New Imperialists: ideologies of empire* (Oxford: Oneworld, 2006), pp. 111–35.
38. Epitomised by Waltz, K., *Theory of International Politics* (Reading, MA & London: Addison-Wesley, 1979); a brief but clear summary, and discussion of its application to Rome, in Eckstein, 'Conceptualizing', pp. 577–80.
39. cf. Doyle, *Empires*, pp. 125–7.
40. Excellent summary in Beard, M. & Crawford, M., *Rome in the Late Republic: problems and interpretations* (London: Duckworth, 2nd edn, 1999), pp. 12–24.
41. Ibid., pp. 53–5.
42. This section is heavily indebted to the ideas of Rosenstein, N., *Rome at War: farms, families and death in the Middle Republic* (Chapel Hill, NC: University of North Carolina Press, 2004).
43. Hopkins, K., 'The political economy of the Roman empire', in Morris & Scheidel (eds), *Dynamics of Ancient Empires*, pp. 178–204.
44. Rich, J., 'The supposed manpower shortage of the lated second century BC', *Historia*, 1983 (32), pp. 287–331.
45. Hopkins, K., *Conquerors and Slaves: sociological studies in Roman history I* (Cambridge: Cambridge University Press, 1978), pp. 1–78; de Ligt, L. & Northwood, S. (eds), *People, Land and Politics: demographic developments and the transformation of Roman Italy, 300 BC – AD 14* (Leiden: Brill, 2008).
46. Rosenstein, *Rome at War*.
47. Morley, N., *Metropolis and Hinterland: the city of Rome and the Italian economy, 200 BC – AD 200* (Cambridge: Cambridge University Press, 1996).
48. Cornell, T.J., 'The end of Roman imperial expansion', in Rich & Shipley (eds), *War and Society*, pp. 139–70.

CHAPTER 2

1. See the account of Palmerston, Gladstone and Disraeli in Vance, N., *The Victorians and Ancient Rome* (Oxford: Blackwell, 1997), pp. 225–32.
2. Hitler cited by Loseman, V., 'The Nazi concept of Rome', in Edwards, C. (ed.), *Roman Presences: receptions of Rome in European culture, 1789–1945* (Cambridge: Cambridge University Press, 1999), pp. 221–35. On Fascist Italy see Store, M., 'A flexible Rome: Fascism and the cult of romanità', in ibid., pp. 205–20.
3. Betts, R.F., 'The allusion to Rome in British imperial thought of the late nineteenth and early twentieth centuries', *Victorian Studies*, 1971 (15), pp. 149–59.
4. Seeley, J.R., *Roman Imperialism: lectures and essays* (London: Macmillan, 1870), p. 31.
5. Haverfield, F., 'An inaugural address delivered before the first Annual General Meeting of the Society', *Journal of Roman Studies*, 1911 (1), p. xviii.
6. Lucas, C.P., *Greater Rome and Greater Britain* (Oxford: Oxford University Press, 1912), p. 12; see generally Bell, D., 'From ancient to modern in Victorian imperial thought', *Historical Journal*, 2006 (49), pp. 735–59.
7. Trevelyan, C., *On the Education of the People of India* (London: Longman, Orme, Brown, Green & Longman, 1838), pp. 196–7.
8. Baring, E., Earl of Cromer, *Ancient and Modern Imperialism* [1910] (Honolulu: University Press of the Pacific, 2001), p. 89; cf. pp. 35–6, 72–3.
9. Bryce, J., *The Ancient Roman Empire and the British Empire in India* (Oxford: Oxford University Press, 1914), pp. 24–5.
10. Seeley, J.R., *The Expansion of England* (London: Macmillan, 1883), p. 305.
11. Robertson, J.M., *Patriotism and Empire* (London: Grant Richards, 1899), e.g. pp. 151–7; the narrative moves directly from Caesar's overthrow of the Republic to Renaissance Florence. Cf. J.A. Hobson's characterisation of the imperialism of Rome, which focuses on the rise of a money-loaning aristocracy, the expropriation of the Italian peasants and the decay of morals, all themes most closely associated with the last century of the Republic; *Imperialism: a study* (London: Allen & Unwin, 1902), p. 365.
12. Mann, M., *The Sources of Social Power Volume I: a history of power from the beginning to AD 1760* (Cambridge: Cambridge University Press, 1986), p. 250.
13. Doyle, M.W., *Empires* (Ithaca: Cornell University Press, 1986), p. 119.
14. Lal, D., *In Praise of Empires: globalization and order* (New York & Basingstoke: Palgrave Macmillan, 2004), pp. xviii–xxii, 33–42. The nineteenth-century European empires seem to be treated as elements in a system of anarchic inter-state competition and hence not as true empires.
15. Thayer, B.A., 'The case for the Roman Empire', in Layne, C. & Thayer, B.A., *American Empire: a debate* (New York & London: Routledge, 2007), p. 42. And see generally Ferguson, N., *Colossus: the price of America's empire* (London: Penguin, 2004).
16. Curchin, L.A., *Roman Spain: conquest and assimilation* (London: Routledge, 1991), pp. 24–54; Richardson, J.S., *The Romans in Spain* (Oxford: Blackwell, 1996), pp. 41–149.
17. Curchin, *Roman Spain*, pp. 35 and 41.

18. Weinstock, S., 'Pax and the "Ara Pacis"', *Journal of Roman Studies*, 1960 (50), pp. 44–58.

19. Woolf, G., 'Roman peace', in Rich, J. & Shipley, G. (eds.), *War and Society in the Roman World* (London & New York: Routledge, 1993), pp. 171–94.

20. MacMullen, R., *Enemies of the Roman Order: treason, unrest and alienation in the Empire* (Cambridge, MA: Harvard University Press, 1967), pp. 192–241; Shaw, B.D., 'Bandits in the Roman Empire', *Past & Present*, 1984 (105), pp. 3–52; Grünewald, T., *Bandits in the Roman Empire: myth and reality* (London & New York: Routledge, 2004); de Souza, P., *Piracy in the Graeco–Roman World* (Cambridge: Cambridge University Press, 1999).

21. Dyson, S.L., 'Native revolt patterns in the Roman Empire', *Aufstieg und Niedergand der Römischer Welt* Vol. II.3 (Berlin & New York: de Gruyter, 1975), pp. 138–75; Pekary, T., 'Seditio: Unruhen und Revolten im Römischen Reich von Augustus bis Commodus', *Ancient Society*, 1987 (18), pp. 133–50.

22. Woolf, 'Roman peace'.

23. Cornell, T., 'The end of Roman imperial expansion', in Rich & Shipley (eds), *War and Society*, pp. 139–70; Whittaker, C.R., *Frontiers of the Roman Empire: a social and economic study* (Baltimore, MD: Johns Hopkins University Press, 1994), pp. 31–97.

24. Woolf, 'Roman peace', pp. 185–9; Brunt, P.A., 'Did imperial Rome disarm her subjects?', in *Roman Imperial Themes* (Oxford: Oxford University Press, 1990), pp. 255–66.

25. On the comparison with China, Hopkins, K., *Death and Renewal: sociological studies in Roman history II* (Cambridge: Cambridge University Press, 1983), p. 186.

26. On the speed of communication, Duncan-Jones, R.P., *Structure and Scale in the Roman Economy* (Cambridge: Cambridge University Press, 1990), pp. 7–8; generally on distance, time and connectivity, Horden, P. & Purcell, N., *The Corrupting Sea: a study of Mediterranean history* (Oxford: Blackwell, 2000).

27. Braund, D. (ed.), *The Administration of the Roman Empire 241 BC – AD 193* (Exeter: Exeter University Press, 1988); Garnsey, P. & Saller, R., *The Roman Empire: economy, society, culture* (London: Duckworth, 1987), pp. 26–34.

28. Lintott, A., *Imperium Romanum: politics and administration* (London & New York: Routledge, 1993), pp. 32–42.

29. Ibid., pp. 146–7.

30. Dench, E., *Romulus' Asylum: Roman identities from the age of Alexander to the age of Hadrian* (Oxford: Oxford University Press, 2005).

31. See for example the *Lex Irnitana* from late first-century CE Spain, table XXI, in Gonzales, J., 'The *Lex Irnitana*: a new copy of the Flavian municipal law', in *Journal of Roman Studies*, 1986 (76), pp. 147–243.

32. Lucas, C.P., *Greater Rome and Greater Britain* (Oxford: Oxford University Press, 1912), pp. 97, 101; Ferguson, *Colossus*, p. 34.

33. Miles, G.B., 'Roman and modern imperialism: a reassessment', *Comparative Studies in Society and History*, 1990 (32), pp. 629–59.

34. Hanson, W.S., 'Forces of change and methods of control', in Mattingly, D.J. (ed.), *Dialogues in Roman Imperialism* (Portsmouth, RI: *Journal of Roman Archaeology* Supplementary Series 23, 1997), pp. 67–80.

35. Alcock, S.E., *Graecia Capta: the landscapes of Roman Greece* (Cambridge: Cambridge University Press, 1993), pp. 129–71.

36. *British Museum Papyrus* 1912, taken from Lewis, N. & Reinhold, M. (eds), *Roman Civilization: selected readings* Vol. 2 (New York: Harper & Row, 3rd edn, 1990), pp. 285–8.

37. Bowman, A.K., *The Town Councils of Roman Egypt* (Toronto: Hakkert, 1971).

38. Hanson, W.S., 'Administration, urbanisation and acculturation in the Roman West', in Braund, *Administration*, pp. 53–68.

39. Wells, P.S., *The Barbarians Speak: how the conquered peoples shaped Roman Europe* (Princeton & Oxford: Princeton University Press, 1999), pp. 114–21.

40. Ibid., pp. 95–8.

41. Lintott, *Imperium Romanum*, pp. 129–30; on Gaul, Woolf, G., *Becoming Roman: the origins of provincial civilization in Gaul* (Cambridge: Cambridge University Press, 1998), pp. 106–41; on Britain, Millett, M., *The Romanization of Britain: an essay in archaeological interpretation* (Cambridge: Cambridge University Press, 1990), pp. 65–126; on Spain, Curchin, L.A., *The Romanization of Central Spain: complexity, diversity and change in a provincial hinterland* (London & New York: Routledge, 2004), pp. 69–95.

42. Generally on the ancient ideology of urbanism, Ramage, E.S., *Urbanitas: ancient sophistication and refinement* (Norman, OK: University of Oklahoma Press, 1973).

43. Cf. Woolf, *Becoming Roman*, pp. 71–2; Lintott, *Imperium Romanum*, pp. 132–45.

44. On modern views of cities as dynamic and civilising agents, see Williams, R., *The Country and the City* (London: Hogarth Press, 1973), and Holton, R.J., *Cities, Capitalism and Civilization* (London: Allen & Unwin, 1986).

45. See for example Finley, M.I., 'The ancient city: from Fustel de Coulanges to Max Weber and beyond', in *Economy and Society in Ancient Greece* (London: Chatto & Windus, 1981), pp. 3–23; Rich, J. & Wallace-Hadrill, A., (eds), *City and Country in the Ancient World* (New York & London: Routledge, 1991).

46. See the papers by P. Abrams in Abrams, P. & Wrigley, E.A., (eds), *Towns in Societies: essays in economic history and historical sociology* (Cambridge: Cambridge University Press, 1978); Castells, M., 'Theory and ideology in urban sociology', in Pickvance, C.G. (ed.), *Urban Sociology: critical essays* (London: Tavistock, 1976), pp. 60–84.

47. This approach draws on the ideas of Eisenstadt, S.N. & Shachar, A., *Society, Culture and Urbanization* (Newbury Park CA: Sage, 1987) and Mann, M., *The Sources of Social Power, Volume I: a history of power from the beginning to A.D. 1760* (Cambridge: Cambridge University Press, 1986). It is developed in more detail for the specific case of Republican Italy in Morley, N., 'Urbanisation and development in Italy in the late Republic', in Northwood S. & de Ligt, L. (eds), *People, Land and Politics: demographic developments and the transformation of Roman Italy, 300 BC – AD 14* (Leiden: Brill, 2008), pp. 121–37.

48. Morley, N., 'Cities in context: urban systems in Roman Italy', in Parkins, H. (ed.), *The Roman City: beyond the consumer model* (London & New York: Routledge, 1997), pp. 42–58.

49. cf. Habinek, T., *The Politics of Latin Literature: writing, identity and empire in ancient Rome* (Princeton: Princeton University Press, 1998), pp. 34–68.

50. Hingley, R., 'Resistance and domination: social change in Roman Britain', in Mattingly (ed.), *Dialogues in Roman Imperialism*, pp. 81–100.

51. Goodman, M., *The Ruling Class of Judaea: the origins of the Jewish revolt against Rome AD 66–70* (Cambridge: Cambridge University Press, 1987).
52. Veyne, P., *Bread and Circuses: historical sociology and political pluralism* (London: Allan Lane, 1990).
53. Lintott, *Imperium Romanum*, pp. 46–52.
54. Ibid., pp. 65–9, 154–60.
55. Macmullen, *Corruption*.
56. Garnsey & Saller, *Roman Empire*, pp. 148–56.
57. Brunt, P.A., 'Princeps and equites', *Journal of Roman Studies*, 1983 (73), pp. 42–75.

CHAPTER 3

1. See generally Mommsen, W.J,. *Theories of Imperialism*, trans. Falla, P.A. (London: Weidenfeld & Nicolson, 1981); Brewer, A., *Marxist Theories of Imperialism: a critical survey* (2nd edn) (London & New York: Routledge, 1990).
2. e.g. Ray, D., *Development Economics* (Princeton, NJ: Princeton University Press, 1998); Smith, C. & Rees, G., *Economic Development* (Basingstoke: Macmillan, 1998).
3. The classic statement is Hobson, J.A., *Imperialism: a study* (London: Allen & Unwin, 1902).
4. Hill, P., *Development Economics on Trial* (Cambridge: Cambridge University Press, 1986).
5. Mommsen, *Theories of Imperialism*, pp. 113–41; Amin, S., *Unequal Development: an essay on the social formations of peripheral capitalism*, trans. Pearce, B. (Hassocks: Harvester, 1976); Harvey, D., *The New Imperialism* (Oxford: Oxford University Press, 2003).
6. e.g. Harvey, *The New Imperialism*; Mooers, C. (ed.), *The New Imperialism: ideologies of empire* (Oxford: Oneworld, 2006); Klein, N., *The Shock Doctrine: the rise of disaster capitalism* (London: Allen Lane, 2007).
7. Smith, A., *An Enquiry into the Nature and Causes of the Wealth of Nations* [1776], Campbell, R.H. & Skinner, A.S. (eds), (Oxford: Oxford University Press, 1976), Section IV.vii.a–b.
8. Steuart, J. *Inquiry into the Principles of Political Economy* [1770] Vol. I (Edinburgh: Scottish Economic Society, 1966), p. 428.
9. Smith, *Wealth of Nations*, Section IV.ix.47.
10. Morley, N., *Antiquity and Modernity* (Oxford & Malden: Wiley-Blackwell, 2009), pp. 21–47.
11. Morley, N., *Theories, Models and Concepts in Ancient History* (London & New York: Routledge, 2004), pp. 33–50.
12. Finley, M.I., *The Ancient Economy* (3rd edn) (Berkeley: University of California Press, 1999).
13. Useful summary in Garnsey, P. & Saller, R., *The Roman Empire: economy, society, culture* (London: Duckworth, 1987), pp. 43–103; some more detailed discussions in Scheidel, W. & von Reden, S. (eds), *The Ancient Economy* (Edinburgh: Edinburgh University Press, 2002).
14. On the organic energy economy of the pre-industrial era, see Wrigley, E.A., *Continuity, Chance and Change: the character of the industrial revolution in England* (Cambridge: Cambridge University Press, 1988).

15. Horden, P. & Purcell, N., *The Corrupting Sea: a study of Mediterranean history* (Oxford: Blackwell, 2000); Morley, N. *Trade in Classical Antiquity* (Cambridge: Cambridge University Press, 2007), pp. 17–34.

16. Saller, R., 'Framing the debate over growth in the ancient economy', in Scheidel & von Reden (eds), *The Ancient Economy*, pp. 251–69.

17. This is the conclusion of the relevant chapters in Scheidel, W., Morris, I. & Saller, R. (eds), *The Cambridge Economic History of the Greco–Roman World* (Cambridge: Cambridge University Press, 2007).

18. See e.g. North, D.C., *Institutions, Institutional Change and Economic Performance* (Cambridge: Cambridge University Press, 1990); Frier, B.W. & Kehoe, D.P., 'Law and economic institutions', in Scheidel, Morris & Saller (eds), *Cambridge Economic History*, pp. 113–43.

19. Hopkins, K., 'The political economy of the Roman empire', in Morris, I. & Scheidel, W. (eds), *The Dynamics of Ancient Empires: state power from Assyria to Byzantium* (Oxford: Oxford University Press. 2009), pp. 178–204; Lo Cascio, E., 'The early Roman empire: the state and the economy', in Scheidel, Morris & Saller (eds), *Cambridge Economic History*, pp. 619–47.

20. Hopkins, K., 'Rome, taxes, rents and trade', in *Kodai* VI/VII, pp. 41–75; reprinted in Scheidel & von Reden (eds), *Ancient Economy*, pp. 190–230.

21. Pliny, *Natural History* 18.35.

22. Andreau, J., *Banking and Business in the Roman World* (Cambridge: Cambridge University Press, 1999).

23. Hopkins, K., 'Models, ships and staples', in Garnsey, P. & Whittaker, C.R. (eds), *Trade and Famine in Classical Antiquity* (Cambridge: Cambridge Philological Society, 1983), pp. 84–109; Garnsey, P., *Famine and Food Supply in the Graeco–Roman World: responses to risk and crisis* (Cambridge: Cambridge University Press, 1988).

24. On *cabotage*, Horden & Purcell, *Corrupting Sea*, pp. 124–72.

25. Whittaker, C.R., *Frontiers of the Roman Empire: a social and economic study* (Baltimore, MD: Johns Hopkins University Press, 1994), pp. 99–104.

26. Erdkamp, P., *Hunger and the Sword: warfare and food supply in Roman republican wars, 264–30 BC* (Amsterdam: J.C. Gieben, 1998); Erdkamp (ed.), *The Roman Army and the Economy* (Amsterdam: J.C. Gieben, 2002).

27. Morley, N., 'The early Roman empire: distribution', in Scheidel, Morris & Saller (eds), *Cambridge Economic History*, pp. 575–6.

28. Morley, N., *Metropolis and Hinterland: the city of Rome and the Italian economy 200 BC – AD 200* (Cambridge: Cambridge University Press, 1996), pp. 33–54.

29. Scheidel, W., 'Demography', in Scheidel, Morris & Saller (eds), *Cambridge Economic History*, pp. 38–86, esp. 74–85.

30. Curchin, L.A., *Roman Spain: conquest and assimilation* (London: Routledge, 1991), pp. 142–5; Wilson, A., 'Timgad and textile production', in Mattingly, D.J. & Salmon, J. (eds), *Economies Beyond Agriculture in the Classical World* (London & New York: Routledge, 2001), pp. 271–96.

31. Woolf, G., *Becoming Roman: the origins of provincial civilization in Gaul* (Cambridge: Cambridge University Press, 1998), pp. 169–205.

32. Purcell, N., 'Wine and wealth in Roman Italy', *Journal of Roman Studies*, 1985 (75), pp. 1–19.

33. Mitchell, S., 'Requisitioned transport in the Roman empire', *Journal of Roman Studies*, 1976 (66), pp. 106–31.

34. Garnsey, *Famine and Food Supply*, pp. 198–243.
35. See the *Digest of Roman Law* 39.4.4.1, 50.6.6.8; Sirks, B., *Food for Rome: the legal structure of the transportation and processing of supplies for the imperial distributions in Rome and Constantinople* (Amsterdam: J.C. Gieben, 1991).
36. cf. Whittaker, C.R., 'Trade and the aristocracy in the Roman empire', *Opus* 4, pp. 49–76.
37. Duncan-Jones, R.P., *The Economy of the Roman Empire: quantitative studies* (2nd edn) (Cambridge: Cambridge University Press, 1982), pp. 345–7.
38. Frayn, J.M., *Markets and Fairs in Roman Italy* (Oxford: Oxford University Press, 1993), pp. 1–11, 101–8.
39. Meiggs, R., *Roman Ostia* (2nd edn) (Oxford: Oxford University Press, 1973); G. Rickman, 'Problems of transport and development of ports', in Giovannini, A. (ed.), *Nourrir la Plèbe* (Basel: Kassle, 1991), pp. 103–15.
40. Laurence, R., *The Roads of Roman Italy: mobility and cultural change* (London & New York: Routledge, 1999).
41. Horden & Purcell, *Corrupting Sea*, pp. 126–30.
42. de Souza, P., *Piracy in the Graeco–Roman World* (Cambridge: Cambridge University Press, 1999).
43. Morley, *Trade in Classical Antiquity*, pp. 58–70.
44. Johnston, D., *Roman Law in Context* (Cambridge: Cambridge University Press, 1999).
45. Generally, Howgego, C., *Ancient History from Coins* (London & New York: Routledge, 1995); Lo Cascio, 'State and economy', pp. 627–30.
46. Hopkins, K., 'Taxes and trade in the Roman empire', *Journal of Roman Studies* 70 (1980), pp. 101–25.
47. See Greene, K., *The Archaeology of the Roman Economy* (London: Batsford, 1986).
48. SEG xvii 828, from Nicomedia in Bithynia; on elite disdain for trade, Morley, *Trade in Classical Antiquity*, pp. 79–89.
49. Greene, K., 'The study of Roman technology: some theoretical considerations', in Scott, E. (ed.), *Theoretical Roman Archaeology: first conference proceedings* (Aldershot: Avebury, 1993), pp. 39–47; Greene, 'Technology and innovation in context: the Roman background to medieval and later developments', *Journal of Roman Archaeology*, 1994 (7), pp. 22–33.
50. Pliny, *Natural History* 18.296; White, K.D., *Roman Farming* (London: Thames & Hudson, 1970), pp. 448–52.
51. Morley, *Metropolis and Hinterland*, pp. 116–17.
52. Mattingly, D.J., 'Olea mediterranea?', *Journal of Roman Archaeology*, 1988 (1), pp. 153–61; A. Wilson, 'Machines, power and the ancient economy', *Journal of Roman Studies*, 2002 (92), pp. 1–32, 12–14 on milling complexes.
53. Peterson, L.H., 'The baker, his tomb, his wife and her breadbasket: the monument of Eurysaces in Rome', *Art Bulletin*, 2003 (85), pp. 230–57.
54. Wilson, 'Machines, power and the ancient economy'; Curchin, L.A., *The Romanization of Central Spain: complexity, diversity and change in a provincial hinterland* (London & New York: Routledge, 2004), pp. 144–50.
55. White, *Roman Farming*, pp. 224–71; Sallares, R., *Ecology of the Ancient Greek World* (London: Duckworth, 1991), pp. 341–6.
56. Shaw, B.D., 'Water and society in the ancient Maghrib', *Antiquités Africaines*, 1984 (20), pp. 121–73.

57. Purcell, N., 'Tomb and suburb', in von Hesberg, H. & Zanker, P. (eds), *Römische Gräberstrassen* (Munich: Bayerische Akademie der Wissenschaften, 1987), pp. 25–41; Morley, *Metropolis and Hinterland*, pp. 83–107.
58. Goodman, P.J., *The Roman City and its Periphery: from Rome to Gaul* (London & New York: Routledge, 2007).
59. Morley, *Metropolis and Hinterland*, pp. 108–42.
60. Sallares, *Ecology*, pp. 313–72.
61. Millett, M., *The Romanization of Britain: an essay in archaeological interpretation* (Cambridge: Cambridge University Press, 1990), pp. 157–80; Leveau, P., 'The western provinces', in Scheidel, Morris & Saller (eds), *Cambridge Economic History*, pp. 650–70.
62. Woolf, *Becoming Roman*, pp. 194–202.
63. Bradley, K.R., *Slavery and Society at Rome* (Cambridge: Cambridge University Press, 1994), pp. 31–56.
64. Scheidel, W., 'Quantifying the sources of slaves in the early Roman empire', *Journal of Roman Studies*, 1997 (87), pp. 156–69; Harris, W.V., 'Demography, geography and the sources of Roman slaves', *Journal of Roman Studies*, 1999 (89), pp. 62–75, argues for 4–8 million.
65. Bradley, *Slavery and Society*, pp. 15–30; Fitzgerald, W., *Slavery and the Roman Literary Imagination* (Cambridge: Cambridge University Press, 2000).
66. Generally on the villa, Carandini, A., *Schiavi in Italia: gli strumenti pensanti dei Romani fra tarda repubblica e medio impero* (Rome: La Nuova Italia Scientifica, 1988).
67. On different aspects of this crisis, see de Ligt, L. & Northwood, S. (eds), *People, Land and Politics: demographic developments and the transformation of Roman Italy, 300 BC – AD 14* (Leiden: Brill, 2008). On modern attitudes to ancient slavery, see Finley, M.I., *Ancient Slavery and Modern Ideology* (London: Chatto & Windus, 1980); Morley, N., *Antiquity and Modernity* (Oxford & Malden, MA: Wiley-Blackwell, 2008), pp. 26–7, 42–3, 150–9.
68. Summarised in Morley, *Metropolis and Hinterland*, pp. 126–9.
69. Joshel, S., *Work, Identity and Legal Status at Rome: a study of the occupational inscriptions* (Norman, OK: University of Oklahoma Press, 1992).
70. On the mechanisms of control, Bradley, K.R., *Slaves and Masters in the Roman Empire: a study in social control* (Brussels: Latomus, 1984).
71. Morley, *Metropolis and Hinterland*, pp. 129–35.
72. Bradley, *Slavery and Society*, pp. 57–80.
73. Bagnall, R. & Frier, B.W., *The Demography of Roman Egypt* (Cambridge: Cambridge University Press, 1994), p. 48.
74. Rathbone, D., *Economic Rationalism and Rural Society in Third-Century AD Egypt* (Cambridge: Cambridge University Press, 1991), pp. 89–91; Rowlandson, J., *Landowners and Tenants in Roman Egypt: the social relations of agriculture in the Oxyrhynchite Nome* (Oxford: Oxford University Press, 1996), p. 205.
75. e.g. Apuleius *Metamorphoses* 7.15–28; Longus, *Daphnis & Chloe* 4.19.
76. Todd, M., *The Early Germans* (2nd edn) (Oxford: Blackwell, 2004), p. 32; Cunliffe, B., *The Ancient Celts* (Oxford: Oxford University Press, 1997), p. 220.
77. Diodorus Siculua 5.38.1, Strabo 3.2.10; Edmondson, J., *Two Industries in Roman Lusitania: mining and garum production* (Oxford: British Archaeological Reports, 1987).

78. Thompson, F.H., *The Archaeology of Greek and Roman Slavery* (London: Duckworth, 2003).

79. Samson, R., 'Rural slavery, inscriptions, archaeology and Marx: a response to Ramsay MacMullen's "Late Roman slavery"', *Historia*, 1989 (38), pp. 99–110; contra. MacMullen, R., 'Late Roman slavery', *Historia*, 1987 (36), pp. 359–82.

80. Woolf, *Becoming Roman*, pp. 148–59.

81. Curchin, L.A., *Roman Spain: conquest and assimilation* (London & New York: Routledge, 1991), pp. 125–9; Thompson, *Archaeology*, pp. 103–30.

82. Tchernia, A., *Le Vin de l'Italie Romaine* (Rome: Ecole Française de Rome, 1986), pp. 172–84.

83. Erdkamp, *Grain Market*, pp. 143–205.

84. Wallerstein, I., *The Modern World-System, Volume I* (New York: Academic Press, 1974); Woolf, G., 'World-systems analysis and the Roman empire', *Journal of Roman Archaeology*, 1990 (3), pp. 44–58.

85. Mann, M., *The Sources of Social Power, Volume I* (Cambridge: Cambridge University Press, 1986), pp. 148–55.

86. Hong, S., et al., 'Greenland ice evidence of hemispheric lead pollution 2 millennia ago by Greek and Roman civilizations', *Science*, 1994 (265), pp. 1841–43; 'A reconstruction of changes in copper production and copper emissions to the atmosphere during the past 7000 years', *The Science of Total Environment*, 1996 (188), pp. 183–93.

87. *Cf.* Grigg, D.B., *Population Growth and Agrarian Change: an historical perspective* (Cambridge: Cambridge University Press, 1980); Scheidel, W., 'Demography', in Scheidel, Morris & Saller (eds), *Cambridge Economic History*, pp. 38–86.

88. Wightman, E.M., 'Peasants and potentates. An investigation of social structures and land tenure in Roman Gaul', *American Journal of Ancient History*, 1978 (3), pp. 97–128; Woolf, *Becoming Roman*, pp. 41–3; Woolf, 'Regional productions in early Roman Gaul', in Mattingly & Salmon (eds), *Economies Beyond Agriculture*, pp. 49–65.

89. Alcock, S.E., *Graecia Capta: the landscapes of Roman Greece* (Cambridge: Cambridge University Press, 1993), pp. 74–83.

90. Curchin, *Roman Spain* and *Romanization of Central Spain*.

91. *Cf.* Morley, *Metropolis and Hinterland*, pp. 143–58, on the development of Apulia and other 'marginal' areas of Italy.

92. Patterson, J.R., 'Crisis: what crisis? Rural change and urban development in imperial Appenine Italy', *Papers of the British School at Rome*, 1987 (55), pp. 115–46; Morley, *Metropolis and Hinterland*, pp. 135–42.

93. McCormick, M., *Origins of the European Economy: communications and commerce AD 300–900* (Cambridge: Cambridge University Press, 2001), pp. 40–1.

94. de Ligt, L., 'Demand, supply, distribution: the Roman peasantry between town and countryside', *Münstersche Beiträge zur antiken Handelsgeschichte*, 1990 (9), pp. 24–56.

95. This is the key argument of Hopkins, 'Taxes and trade' and 'Rome, taxes, rents and trade'.

96. On 'mass luxuries', Morley, *Trade in Classical Antiquity*, pp. 39–49.

97. Garnsey & Saller, *The Roman Empire*, pp. 66–71.

98. Rathbone, D., 'Roman Egypt', in Scheidel, Morris & Saller (eds), *Cambridge Economic History*, pp. 698–719; Jongman, W., 'The early Roman empire: consumption', in ibid., pp. 592–618.

99. Garnsey, P., *Food and Society in Classical Antiquity* (Cambridge: Cambridge University Press, 1999); cf. Fogel, R.W., *The Escape from Hunger and Premature Death, 1700–2100: Europe, America and the Third World* (Cambridge: Cambridge University Press, 2004).

100. cf. Morley, N., 'The poor in the city of Rome', in Atkins, M. & Osborne, R. (eds), *Poverty in the Roman World* (Cambridge: Cambridge University Press, 2006), pp. 21–39.

101. Morley, N., 'Markets, marketing and the Roman elite', in Lo Cascio, E. (ed.), *Mercati Periodici e Mercati Permanenti nel mondo romano* (Rome & Bari: Edipuglia, 2000), pp. 211–21.

CHAPTER 4

1. But *apart* from all that ...? Monty Python, *Life of Brian*, 1979.

2. Seeley, J.R., *The Expansion of England* (London: Macmillan, 1883), pp. 238–9.

3. Huntington, S.P., *The Clash of Civilizations and the Remaking of World Order* (New York: Simon & Schuster, 1996), pp. 69–70.

4. Montgomery, W.F., 'The imperial ideal', in Goldman, C.S. (ed.), *The Empire and the Century* (London: John Murray, 1905), pp. 5–28; quote from p. 7.

5. Mattingly, D., 'From one colonialism to another: imperialism and the Maghreb', in Webster, J. & Cooper, N. (eds), *Roman imperialism: post-colonial perspectives* (Leicester: Leicester Archaeology Monographs, 1996), pp. 49–70; Terrenato, N., 'Ancestor cults: the perception of ancient Rome in modern Italian culture', in Hingley, R. (ed.), *Images of Rome: perceptions of ancient Rome in Europe and the United States in the modern age* (Portsmouth, RI: *Journal of Roman Archaeology* Supplementary Series 44, 2001), pp. 71–89.

6. *The Expansion of England* (London: Macmillan, 1883), p. 253.

7. Hingley, R., *Roman Officers and English Gentlemen: the imperial origins of Roman archaeology* (London & New York: Routledge, 2000).

8. Montgomery, 'The imperial ideal', p. 7.

9. Lucas, C.P., *Greater Rome and Greater Britain* (Oxford: Oxford University Press, 1912), p. 94.

10. Haverfield, F., 'An inaugural address delivered before the first Annual General Meeting of the Society', *Journal of Roman Studies*, 1911 (1), pp. xi–xx; quote from p. xvii.

11. Baring, E., Earl of Cromer, *Ancient and Modern Imperialism* [1910] (Honolulu: University Press of the Pacific, 2001), p. 89.

12. Lucas, *Greater Rome*, p. 97; Bryce, J., *The Ancient Roman Empire and the British Empire in India* (Oxford: Oxford University Press, 1914), pp. 58–9.

13. Bryce, *Ancient Roman Empire*, p. 41.

14. Sinopoli, C.M., 'Imperial integration and imperial subjects', in Alcock, S.E., et al. (eds), *Empires: perspectives from archaeology and history* (Cambridge: Cambridge University Press, 2001), pp. 195–200.

15. Doyle, M.W., *Empires* (Ithaca, NY: Cornell University Press, 1986), pp. 92–8.

16. Mann, M., *The Sources of Social Power* Vol. I (Cambridge: Cambridge University Press, 1986), pp. 250–300.

17. Rostovtzeff, M.I., *A History of the Ancient World* Vol. I, trans. Duff, J.M., (Oxford: Oxford University Press, 1926), p. 10.

18. On the history of scholarship, see Freeman, P.W.M., 'Mommsen through to Haverfield: the origins of Romanization studies in late 19th-c. Britain', in Mattingly, D.W. (ed.), *Dialogues in Roman Imperialism: power, discourse, and discrepant experience in the Roman Empire* (Portsmouth, RI: *Journal of Roman Archaeology* Supplementary Series 23, 1997), pp. 27–50; Hingley, R., *Globalizing Roman Culture: unity, diversity and empire* (London & New York: Routledge, 2005), pp. 14–48.

19. Haverfield, F., *The Romanization of Roman Britain* (4th edn) (Oxford: Oxford University Press, 1923), p. 22.

20. Freeman, P.W.M., 'British imperialism and the Roman empire', in Webster & Cooper (eds), *Roman Imperialism*, pp. 19–34.

21. Woolf, G., *Becoming Roman* (Cambridge: Cambridge University Press, 1998), pp. 4–7.

22. Haverfield, *Romanization*, p. 10.

23. Mattingly, D., 'Introduction', in Mattingly (ed.), *Dialogues in Roman Imperialism*, p. 9.

24. cf. Hingley, R., 'Resistance and domination: social change in Roman Britain', in Mattingly (ed.), *Dialogues in Roman Imperialism*, pp. 81–100.

25. See the papers in Webster & Cooper (eds), *Roman Imperialism*. Generally on post-colonial theory, see Young, R.J.C., *White Mythologies: writing history and the West* (London & New York: Routledge, 1990); Said, E., *Culture and Imperialism* (London: Vintage, 1993); Loomba, A., *Colonialism/Postcolonialism* (London & New York: Routledge 1998); Chakrabarty, D., *Provincialising Europe: postcolonial thought and historical difference* (Princeton, NJ: Princeton University Press, 2001). There is an outline summary and discussion in Bush, B., *Imperialism and Postcolonialism* (Harlow: Pearson, 2006).

26. Millett, M., *The Romanization of Britain* (Cambridge: Cambridge University Press, 1990); Woolf, *Becoming Roman*. Discussed by Hingley, R., *Globalizing Roman Culture*, pp. 40–8.

27. cf. Morley, N., *Trade in Classical Antiquity* (Cambridge: Cambridge University Press, 2007), pp. 36–49 on theories of consumption.

28. Terrenato, N., 'Introduction' and 'A tale of three cities: the Romanization of northern coastal Etruria', in Keay, S. & Terrenato, N. (eds), *Italy and the West: comparative issues in Romanization* (Oxford: Oxbow, 2001), pp. 1–6, 54–67.

29. cf. Hingley, 'Resistance and domination'.

30. Generally, Mattingly (ed.), *Dialogues in Roman Imperialism*.

31. Barrett, J.C., 'Romanization: a critical comment', in Mattingly (ed.), *Dialogues in Roman Imperialism*, pp. 51–64.

32. Kain, P.J., *Schiller, Hegel and Marx: state, society and the aesthetic ideal of ancient Greece* (Kingston & Montreal: McGill-Queen's University Press, 1982); Williams, R., *Keywords: a vocabulary of culture and society* (London: Fontana, 1983), pp. 89–90.

33. Wallace-Hadrill, A., 'Rome's cultural revolution', *Journal of Roman Studies*, 1989 (79), pp. 157–64; Habinek, T.N. & Schiesaro, A. (eds), *The Roman Cultural Revolution* (Cambridge: Cambridge University Press, 1997); Habinek,

T.N., *The Politics of Latin Literature: writing, identity, and empire in ancient Rome* (Princeton, NJ: Princeton University Press, 1998).

34. Woolf, G., 'The Roman cultural revolution in Gaul', in Keay & Terrenato (eds), *Italy and the West*, pp. 173–86.

35. Edwards, C. & Woolf, G. (eds), *Rome the Cosmopolis* (Cambridge: Cambridge University Press, 2003).

36. Barrett, J.C., 'Romanization: a critical comment', in Mattingly (ed.), *Dialogues in Roman Imperialism*, pp. 51–64.

37. Mann, *Sources of Social Power*, pp. 22–4; Ando, C., *Imperial Ideology and Provincial Loyalty in the Roman Empire* (Berkeley, Los Angeles & London: University of California Press, 2000), p. 5.

38. Zanker, P., *The Power of Images in the Age of Augustus*, trans. Shapiro, A. (Ann Arbor, MI: University of Michigan Press, 1988); Wallace-Hadrill, 'Rome's cultural revolution'.

39. Whittaker, C.R., 'Imperialism and culture: the Roman initiative', in Mattingly (ed.), *Dialogues in Roman Imperialism*, pp. 143–63.

40. e.g. Beard, M., North, J. & Price, S., *Religions of Rome* Vol. II (Cambridge: Cambridge University Press, 1998), p. 225.

41. Aelius Aristides, *Oration* 26.10.

42. Woolf, G., 'Inventing empire in ancient Rome', in Alcock, S.E., et al. (eds), *Empires*, pp. 311–22.

43. Ando, *Imperial Ideology*, pp. 49–70.

44. Aristides, *Oration* 26.59; Dench, E., *Romulus' Asylum: Roman identities from the age of Alexander to the age of Hadrian* (Oxford: Oxford University Press, 2005).

45. *Republic* I.40.

46. Ando, *Imperial Ideology*, pp. 350–61.

47. Ibid., pp. 206–73.

48. Beard, North & Price, *Religions of Rome* Vol. I, pp. 348–63.

49. e.g. *IGR* IV.353 from Pergamum, quoted in Beard, North & Price, *Religions of Rome* Vol. II, pp. 255–6.

50. Generally on the role of the emperor in administration, Millar, F., *The Emperor in the Roman World (31 BC – AD 337)* (London: Duckworth, 1977), with Hopkins, K., *Death and Renewal: sociological studies in Roman history II* (Cambridge: Cambridge University Press, 1983) and on the later empire, Kelly, C., *Ruling the Later Roman Empire* (Cambridge, MA: Belknap Press, 2004).

51. Revell, L., *Roman Imperialism and Local Identities* (Cambridge: Cambridge University Press, 2009).

52. Whittaker, 'Imperialism and culture', pp. 144–8.

53. Edwards, C., *The Politics of Immorality in Ancient Rome* (Cambridge: Cambridge University Press, 1993); Berry, C.J., *The Idea of Luxury: a conceptual and historical investigation* (Cambridge: Cambridge University Press, 1994); Morley, N., 'Political economy and classical antiquity', *Journal of the History of Ideas*, 1998 (26), pp. 95–114.

54. Hingley, *Globalizing*, pp. 91–116.

55. cf. Morley, N., 'The poor in the city of Rome', in Atkins, M. & Osborne, R. (eds), *Poverty in the Roman World* (Cambridge: Cambridge University Press, 2006), pp. 21–39.

56. King, A., 'The Romanization of diet in western Europe', in Keay & Terrenato (eds), *Italy and the West*, pp. 210–23.

57. Generally, Swain, S., *Hellenism and Empire: language, classicism and power in the Greek world, AD 50–250* (Oxford: Oxford University Press, 1996).

58. Gruen, E.S., *Culture and National Identity in Republican Rome* (Ithaca, NY: Cornell University Press, 1992).

59. *Epistles*, 2.1.156.

60. Whitmarsh, T., *Greek Literature and the Roman Empire: the politics of imitation* (Oxford: Oxford University Press, 2001).

61. Alcock, S.E., 'The reconfiguration of memory in the eastern Roman empire', in Alcock et al. (eds), *Empires*, pp. 323–50.

62. Beard, North & Price, *Religions of Rome*, pp. 313–48; Revell, *Roman Imperialism*, pp. 110–49.

63. Rüpke, J., 'Urban religion and imperial expansion: priesthoods in the Lex Ursonensis', in de Blois, L., Funke, P. & Hahn, J. (eds), *The Impact of Imperial Rome on Religions, Ritual and Religious Life in the Roman Empire* (Leiden & Boston: Brill, 2006), pp. 11–23.

64. *Inscriptions of Roman Britain* 309, quoted in Champion, C. (ed.), *Roman Imperialism: readings and sources* (Oxford: Blackwell, 2004), p. 265.

65. Webster, J. 'A negotiated syncretism: readings on the development of Romano–Celtic religion', in Mattingly (ed.), *Dialogues in Roman Imperialism*, pp. 165–84.

66. Woolf, 'Roman cultural revolution', pp. 176–8.

67. This section draws heavily on the ideas of Grewal, D.S. *Network Power: the social dynamics of globalization* (New Haven & London: Cornell University Press, 2008).

68. Grewal, *Network Power*, pp. 71–88 on language as standards.

69. Hingley, *Globalizing*, pp. 94–100; Morgan, T., *Literate Education in the Hellenistic and Roman Worlds* (Cambridge: Cambridge University Press, 1998).

ENVOI

1. Ignatieff, M., *Empire Lite: nation-building in Bosnia, Kosovo and Afghanistan* (London: Vintage, 2003), p. 3.

2. On the decline and fall of the Roman Empire, see Womersley, D., *The Transformation of the Decline and Fall of the Roman Empire* (Cambridge: Cambridge University Press, 1988).

3. Berry, C.J., *The Idea of Luxury: a conceptual and historical investigation* (Cambridge: Cambridge University Press, 1994).

4. Morley, N., *Antiquity and Modernity* (Oxford & Malden: Wiley-Blackwell, 2008).

5. Simonde de Sismondi, J.C.L., *Nouvelles principes de l'économie politique* [1819] Vol. II (2nd edn) (Paris: Delaunay, 1827), p. 434; Hegel, G.W.F., *Vorlesungen über die Philosophie der Geschichte* [1840], in *Werke* Vol. 12 (Frankfurt: Suhrkamp Verlag, 1970), p. 17.

6. Haverfield, F., 'An inaugural address delivered before the first Annual General Meeting of the Society', *Journal of Roman Studies*, 1911 (1), pp. xi–xx; Bell, D.S., 'From ancient to modern in Victorian imperial thought', *Historical Journal*, 2006 (49), pp. 735–59.

7. Morley, *Antiquity and Modernity*, pp. 4–5, 9–17.

8. 'Conjectures on the beginning of human history', in Reiss, H. (ed.), *Political Writings* (2nd edn), trans. Nisbet, R. (Cambridge: Cambridge University Press, 1991), p. 228 note.

9. Wolfreys, J., *Victorian Hauntings: spectrality, Gothic, the uncanny, and literature* (Basingstoke: Palgrave Macmillan, 2001); N. Morley, 'Decadence as a theory of history', *New Literary History*, 2004 (35), pp. 573–85.

10. Edwards, C., *Writing Rome: textual approaches to the city* (Cambridge: Cambridge University Press, 1996), pp. 69–95, and Edwards, C. (ed.), *Roman Presences: receptions of Rome in European culture, 1789–1945* (Cambridge: Cambridge University Press, 1999)

11. Speech at the anniversary of the *People's Paper*, in Marx, K.H, *Collected Works* XIV (London: Lawrence & Wishart, 1980); Morris, W., *News from Nowhere: or, an epoch of Rest* (London: Longmans, Green, 1892).

12. Rostovtzeff, M.I., *A History of the Ancient World* Vol. I, trans. Duff, J.M., (Oxford: Oxford University Press, 1926), p. 541.

13. Berman, M., *The Twilight of American Culture* (New York: W.W. Norton, 2000); quote from p. 30.

14. Piganiol, A., *L'Empire Chrétien (325–395)* (Paris: Presses Universitaires de France, 1947), p. 422; Nye Jr, R.S., *Soft Power: the means to success in world politics* (New York: World Affairs, 2004), p. x.

15. e.g. Westermann, W.L., 'The economic basis of the decline of ancient culture' [1915], reprinted in Kagan, D. (ed.), *Decline and Fall of the Roman Empire: why did it collapse?* (Boston, MA: D.C. Heath, 1962), pp. 32–43.

16. e.g. Boak, A.E.R., 'Manpower shortage and the fall of Rome' [1955], in Kagan (ed.), *Decline and Fall of the Roman Empire*, pp. 23–31; Frank, T., 'Race mixture in the Roman empire' [1916], in the same volume, pp. 44–56.

17. 'Speech delivered at the First All-Union Congress of Collective-Farm Shock Brigades, 19th February 1933', in *Works* Vol. 13 (London: Lawrence & Wishart, 1955), p. 245.

18. Gowing, A., *Empire and Memory: the representation of the Roman republic in imperial culture* (Cambridge: Cambridge University Press, 2005).

19. MacMullen, R., *Corruption and the Decline of Rome* (New Haven & London: Yale University Press, 1988), p. 1.

20. Marx, K., *Die achtzehnte Brumaire des Louis Bonaparte* [1852], in *Marx–Engels Werke* Vol. 8 (Berlin: Dietz, 1960), p. 115.

21. Ibid., p. 117.

Index